Madame La Mort
and Other Plays

PAJ BOOKS

*Bonnie Marranca
and Gautam Dasgupta
Series Editors*

TRANSLATED
AND EDITED BY
KIKI GOUNARIDOU
AND FRAZER LIVELY

INTRODUCTION BY
FRAZER LIVELY

RACHILDE
Madame La Mort
and Other Plays

THE JOHNS HOPKINS
UNIVERSITY PRESS
BALTIMORE AND LONDON

Introduction and English translation
© 1998 The Johns Hopkins University Press
All rights reserved. Published 1998
Printed in the United States of America
on acid-free paper
07 06 05 04 03 02 01 00 99 98   5 4 3 2 1

In French: *La Voix du sang* and *Madame la Mort*
originally appeared in *Théâtre* in 1891;
Volupté and *Le Rôdeur* in *Mercure de France,* 1893;
La Femme peinte in *Mercure de France,* 1 August
1921; and *La Poupée transparente* in *Le Monde
Nouveau,* 20 March 1919. Copyright Edith Silve.

Performance rights in English: Kiki Gounaridou
and Frazer Lively, c/o Department of Theatre
Studies, Cathedral of Learning 1617, University
of Pittsburgh, Pittsburgh, Pa. 15260

The Johns Hopkins University Press
2715 North Charles Street
Baltimore, Maryland 21218-4319
The Johns Hopkins Press Ltd., London

Library of Congress Cataloging-in-Publication
Data will be found at the end of this book.
A catalog record for this book is available from
the British Library.

ISBN 0-8018-5761-9, ISBN 0-8018-5762-7 (pbk.)

Frontispiece: after portrait of Rachilde by
unknown artist. Photo on p. 2: Rachilde ca. 1900.
Bibliothèque Littéraire Jacques Doucet.

TO CORNELIA LIVELY IZEN, SARA MAYES LIVELY,
AND XANTHIPPE GOUNARIDOU

Contents

Acknowledgments

THIS IS AN ANTHOLOGY OF PLAYS BY RACHILDE, ONCE A very popular French woman writer, who has been all but forgotten as a playwright. The recovery of plays, letters, manuscripts, pictures, and reviews would have been impossible without considerable assistance. We gratefully acknowledge the help of the many people who made this collection possible.

Frazer Lively received material assistance to do research in Paris through a grant from the Women's Studies Department at the University of Pittsburgh, a dissertation award from the American Society for Theatre Research, a Foreign Language Area Studies fellowship from the U.S. Department of Education, and travel funds from the Theatre Arts Department at the University of Pittsburgh. Funding to complete the work included a Provost Fellowship and an Owens Fellowship from the University of Pittsburgh.

Laurence Senelick suggested Rachilde as a research topic and gave repeated encouragement and advice. Dennis Kennedy's seminar on the European avant-garde inspired an interest in the symbolist aesthetic and offered valuable criticism. The Modern Language Association, the American Society for Theatre Research, and the Midwest Theatre Colloquium welcomed the papers that formed the basis for the introduction to this volume. The project was further encouraged and refined by Joseph Donahue, Sheila Stowell, Joel Kaplan, Katherine Kelly, Benjamin Hicks, Attilio Favorini, Mrea Csorba, Michel Corvin, and Tracy Davis. Letters from Jennifer Birkett, Roger Shattuck, Daniel Gerould, and Frantisek Deak helped point the way to the appropriate French archives. Virginia Scott gave useful practical advice on living in Paris.

In Paris, Melanie C. Hawthorne, Christian Laucou, Richard Shryock, and Edith Silve shared their friendship and hospitality, as well as their expertise on Rachilde and the symbolists. Romana Severini welcomed interviews with warmth and generosity. The most valuable repository of Rachilde's papers is the Bibliothèque Littéraire Jacques Doucet. Among the many French librarians who helped make sense of the sometimes formidable Paris archives, thanks are especially due to Mlles Tourniac, Drouin, and Giteau of the Bibliothèque de l'Arsénal, Mme Odile Gigou of the Bibliothèque Historique de la Ville de Paris, Mme Prévert of the manuscript department at the Bibliothèque National, and the curator of the Société des Auteurs et Compositeurs Dramatiques.

Valuable help with translations came from Linda Rouillard (French), Lars Kristiansen (Norwegian), and Marie Baird (Dutch). We give warm personal thanks to Claire Guthuix, Ann Hileman, Ellen Leverenz, Eveline Maréchal, Jeffrey Schlesinger, Deborah Waterkotte, the graduate students in theater at the University of Pittsburgh, and the residents of the Foyer la Vigie. Special thanks to Marc Graham, Lori Messenger, and Joel Tansey, who read and commented on our translations and supported us and our work.

Madame La Mort
and Other Plays

Introduction

FRAZER LIVELY

MANY SYMBOLISTS IN TURN-OF-THE-CENTURY FRANCE
equated "woman" with "nature" and despised both.[1] Paris theater
in the 1890s was nearly closed to women playwrights. A partial
exception was Rachilde (pseudonym of Marguerite Eymery Vallette, 1860–1953). The only woman writer who really belonged to
the French symbolist theater clique, Rachilde cultivated a scan-
dalous persona and wrote decadent novels that disrupted gender
expectations. "A pornographer, well and good! But so very distinguished," said an older writer when he met the adventurous young
woman.[2] Rachilde's fiction is hardly pornographic by modern
standards. Feminist and cultural critics, in the process of reevaluat-
ing her novels, have shown how Rachilde's interest in power and
desire took an approach that was less carnal than cerebral (her
favorite term for her own writing).[3] In her bohemian youth,

though, Rachilde acquired—and perhaps relished—the image of a monster.

Rachilde's career in the theater is hardly known, since critics have concentrated on her fiction. She hosted a salon that attracted the foremost literary figures of the French symbolist movement as well as international celebrities (Oscar Wilde, Kipling, H. G. Wells, and Nietzsche were among her visitors). Up-and-coming younger writers such as Colette and Alfred Jarry received encouragement from Rachilde's three decades of idiosyncratic book reviews. As Jarry's closest friend, Rachilde supported him financially and emotionally, and she persuaded Lugné-Poe to produce *Ubu roi,* the play that made Jarry famous. Her testimony on the audience response to *Ubu*'s opening night gave a skewed account, which is the source of an enduring, false legend among theater historians.[4] Rachilde's encouragement behind the scenes helped assure the existence of the first art theaters in Europe, the Théâtre d'Art and the Théâtre de l'Oeuvre.

Rachilde wrote more than twenty plays, which were produced in Paris, Russia, Germany, Belgium, Denmark, and Norway— plays that were famous among the earliest attempts at nonrealistic drama. She may have been the first to use the term *absurd* for the new styles. Yet she seems to have doubted herself as a playwright. She once wrote, "When people tell me I have talent, I immediately feel a sort of crumpling of myself, a shiver of the spirit, which insists that it is not of me, but of the Other that they speak."[5] For most symbolists, women existed in art as the Other, an invention to fuel masculine notions of female power, helplessness, or perversity. Rachilde obeyed the gender stereotypes of her milieu. She called herself an antifeminist even though she peopled much of her writing with strong women and passive men. Yet she had an influence on the new styles that sparked the beginning of modern theater.

Her life, rich with studied eccentricity, was itself a conscious theatrical product. Rachilde's various memoirs give conflicting stories about her youth. She was born Marguerite Eymery in 1860, the only child of a pianist and of a soldier who was the illegitimate son of an aristocrat. The French defeat in the Franco-Prussian war, in 1870, left its mark on the girl, who hated Germans for the rest of her life. After the war, Marguerite and her parents settled near Périgeux, where her maternal grandfather's newspaper supported the family. Marguerite's great-grandfather had left the priesthood during the French Revolution. Superstition held that all the descendants of a married priest turned into werewolves once a year; Rachilde later enjoyed calling herself a "*loup-garou*," one who would never belong to humankind.

Family tension must have contributed to Marguerite's sense of separation. In one version of her past, she said that her father drank heavily and that he was a Casanova who had paid court to her grandmother before marrying her mother, whom he beat until Marguerite was old enough to tear the whip from his hands. Other accounts say that she identified with her father and hated her elegant mother, a piano teacher who let a pet monkey practice on the keys but wouldn't allow her "slug" of a daughter near the instrument, since the little girl had a pronounced limp and couldn't keep her dresses clean. Marguerite's father made it obvious that he would have preferred a son. She said she was raised as a boy, began to ride horses at the age of four, and went on hunts. Her mother's maternal mask and emotional imbalance left her daughter forever mistrustful of women. Her education was haphazard, but she found refuge in her grandfather's library (which reportedly included the works of the Marquis de Sade). She said later that she "became possessed with a mania for writing" at the age of eight.[6]

Marguerite's parents arranged a marriage with one of her

father's officers when she was fourteen, but according to her memoirs she tried to drown herself in a pond to avoid the match, and the engagement was dropped. It is curious that a photograph of the couple from a private album shows the two arm in arm, the young girl with an expression of exuberant happiness. Perhaps her fiancé jilted her. In any event, for the next several years she devoted herself to writing fiction (and at least one novice play) and began to publish in the local provincial newspapers under assumed names. Her father read some of the stories out loud to the family, carefully censoring passages he considered unsuitable for a young girl to hear. At seventeen, Marguerite wrote to the idolized Victor Hugo for advice and received a brief reply—"Thanks and applause. Courage, Mademoiselle"[7]—which she took as a sign that she was destined for a career as a professional writer.

At around the same time, she took the name Rachilde, which was to become not just a pseudonym but a new identity. At first she said that this was the name of a Swedish nobleman who had contacted her during a séance, but later she admitted that she had knocked on the table at random as a hoax. Her gullible and increasingly unstable mother (who was to spend part of her life as an inmate at Charenton, the mental asylum outside Paris) would eventually cause difficulty with publishers by insisting that the fictitious nobleman, not Rachilde, was the real author of her books.

When she turned twenty-one, in 1881, Rachilde moved permanently to Paris, determined to make a living as a writer. Through a cousin, she found work writing articles on ladies' fashion. Soon after she arrived in the capital, she became part of various avant-garde literary circles, including the crowd who called themselves symbolists or "decadents," taking pride in what had originally been a term of insult. At first Rachilde failed to earn much through her writing, even though one novel met with some critical success; but her novel *Monsieur Vénus* (*Mr. Venus*) became a *succès de scandale* when it was published in Belgium in 1884, and the author was given a prison sentence in absentia. For the French edition, Rachilde's friend Maurice Barrès wrote a preface that titillated the general public with the revelation that the novel had been written by an innocent, unmarried young woman. Rachilde gained immediate notoriety. Her Tuesday salon became the place for young literary people to meet, and symbolist poets called her the "queen of the decadents," "Mademoiselle Baudelaire," the "Marquise de Sade." She maintained an aura of personal innocence, but respectable hostesses refused to receive her, in spite of her bourgeois background. Rachilde continued to write best-selling fiction, much of which concerned sexuality, gender reversals, and death.

The construction of her image had begun. She later wrote that at the age of twenty-five she cut her hair short and dyed it blonde.[8] Even more scandalously, she applied to the police for permission to wear men's clothes in public. She justified the need for men's clothing, as George Sand had done the generation before, by her poverty and the flimsiness of expensive women's clothes. She told the police that in her capacity as a journalist who frequented sordid bohemian haunts she would feel safer in male attire. All this may have been true, but cross-dressing would also have made Rachilde look like the mannish female protagonist from *Monsieur Vénus.* Jennifer Birkett writes that Rachilde "found a market and packaged herself for it . . . the man's suit was a statement of intent."[9] During the 1880s her calling card read, "Rachilde, Man of Letters." Many fellow symbolists addressed her as "brother writer" instead of "Mademoiselle." Yet men wrote love sonnets to her pale green eyes and her unconquerable virginity. She wore men's clothes at least once, but she also masqueraded in an eighteenth-century marquise's dress and appeared in costumes like a baby doll short skirt (with her partner

Jean Lorrain dressed as a wrestler, wearing almost nothing). Lorrain, one of her closest friends, infuriated her when he published an article that called her "Mademoiselle Salamander." He opened with the question "*Couche-t-elle?*" (Does she go to bed?). The article concluded that she didn't. Lorrain said Rachilde's novel *La Marquise de Sade* showed she was "completely ignorant of even the alphabet of the physical sensations of love; it is ardently imagined, but not at all lived."[10]

Rachilde's dramatic attempt to parlay her own image to make a splash in the male-dominated literary pond of fin-de-siècle Paris raises fascinating questions. Much of what Rachilde wrote about herself is not to be believed; one near-relative remembers that she "made up incredible lies."[11] Did she really dress as a man? There are artists' renderings and at least one photograph which show her in men's clothes, but a Paris police report from 1884 says that she was refused the permission she sought. M. Puybaraud, the superintendent of police, wrote a careful description of his "stupefying conversation" with the young lady, who appeared to him "more boyish than feminine" and who cheerfully admitted that in writing *Monsieur Vénus,* "I prostituted my pen . . . but my body is intact, and I don't have to blush in front of my mother."[12] According to Puybaraud, Rachilde fully accepted his refusal to bend the stringent French law, which permitted women to wear men's clothes only for reasons of health. But not long afterwards she appeared at a ball in the illegal garb of a dandy. One biographer says that Puybaraud reminded her of the law and she never again repeated the crime of publicly dressing as a man. Another biographer wrote that the prefect of police did authorize her to wear men's suits.[13]

Whatever the literal truth, cross-dressing became part of Rachilde's mystique in the 1880s. She was wearing a man's suit at a ball in 1885 when she met Alfred Vallette. He disapproved of her novels and her social pyrotechnics, which included slapping a man for insulting an actress friend. After a rocky courtship, during which she broke off communication for a year, they married in 1889. She promptly let her hair grow back and stopped going out in public in men's clothing. Her new calling card read, "Rachilde, Madame Alfred Vallette." Her only child was born the next year. Literati stopped speculating about whether Rachilde was a virgin, and her first biographer wrote, "the legend of the Amazon died away on the threshold of the hearth. The story of Rachilde became no more than the history of her books."[14]

But Rachilde refused to settle comfortably into the role of bourgeois wife. She told the editor of *La Plume* that she was still Rachilde, not Madame Vallette, even though the journal was now delivered to a shared apartment. She disliked motherhood and lavished her affection on the rats, mice, and cats she kept as pets. She put her energy into the *Mercure de France,* the literary journal that Vallette helped revive in 1890. She now held her salon at the newspaper; her connections and reputation helped the *Mercure* succeed as the premier avant-garde journal out of the hundreds of small periodicals then circulating in Paris. One of the goals of the *Mercure* was to foster a symbolist theater, a theater of the soul, where the corporeal would be less important than a mystical inner life.

Rachilde wrote her first two plays for the Théâtre d'Art, the art theater founded by the young poet Paul Fort in November 1890. Fort's project would have been inconceivable without the example of André Antoine's Théâtre Libre (Free Theatre), which had just created a sensation in Paris with its new, realistic staging. Subscription audiences marveled at the acting, which seemed close to real life, and at scenery like a butcher shop with actual dripping carcasses of beef. Antoine introduced Ibsen to Paris with his production of *Ghosts,* and he experimented with other serious foreign works, but the staple of the Théâtre Libre repertoire was the short,

gritty play that showed a slice of life in fifteen minutes. These
"*quarts d'heure*" often pictured violent situations from the working
class. Oscar Méténier, one of Antoine's first playwrights, went on
to found the Grand Guignol theater, which specialized in realistic
depictions of torture and pain.

The naturalist plays and production style at the Théâtre Libre
breathed fresh air into a tired medium. The commercial theater in
Paris at the turn of the century showed "digestive plays"[15] to "a
public of ruminants, endlessly chewing the same fodder."[16] The
technical marvels of the nineteenth-century illusionist stage served
plays that dwelt on the theme of marital infidelity. The plot struc-
tures tended to be mechanical, providing little inspiration to spectators. The symbolists rejected this "boulevard" theater, but they
also despised what they saw as the naturalist theater's over-empha-
sis on sordid reality. Realistic sets and even the bodies and voices
of live actors could interfere with achieving a state of reverie. How,
then, could one produce a play in the theater? Mallarmé and
Maeterlinck theorized that a personal response to poetry eclipsed
any attempt at physical realization on stage and that therefore
reading great plays at home was preferable to seeing them live.
What would later constitute a symbolist playing style had yet to be
discovered.

Maeterlinck agreed with Mallarmé that the theater ought to be
a "temple of dreams." Art should speak obliquely, not face to face.
The "mystic density of a work of art" would always disappear
when performed by living actors.[17] Maeterlinck was one of the
best symbolist playwrights, but he refused to let his first play be
produced in the theater, and for a time he resisted having any of
his works staged. He envisioned his dramas as plays for mari-
onettes. Actors, if they appeared at all, should be unimportant
cogs in the combination of music, words, and visual art which
might express the inner essence of the unknown.

If it had not been for the leadership of Paul Fort, the symbolist plays might have remained purely literary pieces, perhaps recited aloud by poets, but never staged by actors. Fort was still a high school student when he began to hang, star-struck, on the outskirts of the crowd at the Café Voltaire, listening to the "learned hullabaloo" of the symbolist poets as they argued against Naturalism. He was transported by "the dazzling beauty of Madame Rachilde" and said that the Voltaire "bubbled every evening like a volcano." One night, Rachilde's husband Alfred Vallette let fall a few words: "What this movement lacks is a theater."[18] At seventeen, Fort gave up his own poetry and left school in order to found and direct this theater.

Fort's Théâtre d'Art was a fusion of the Théâtre Mixte ("mixed," perhaps to show Fort's intended eclecticism) and his friend Louis Germain's Théâtre Idéaliste, which never produced a play. The Théâtre d'Art never had its own home; Fort rented a separate hall for each production, which usually ran no more than two evenings. Between 1890 and 1892 the Théâtre d'Art presented eight programs. The programs generally involved at least two plays and several recitations of poems. In one seventeen-month period, the Théâtre d'Art produced more than twenty plays, each play different from the last; if there was a particular symbolist aesthetic, it was difficult to define. The performances sometimes lasted until the early morning hours, and often ended in a brawl over literary style (a far cry from Mallarmé's vision of a hushed audience who would treat the theater like a temple).

The Théâtre d'Art faced a number of difficulties: shortage of money, neophyte actors, grandiose plans, and largely hostile criticism from the mainstream press, which tended to vilify everything that didn't fit preconceived notions of theater. The biggest lack was a new repertory. Fort had founded his theater with the promise to produce plays by "the young," but in fact there was not

a host of scripts waiting to be staged, and his friends had to
scramble to write some. New styles of performance had yet to be
created. Nevertheless, Fort found visionary artists and writers.
Bonnard, Vuillard, Maurice Denis, Paul Sérusier, Odilon Redon,
and Gauguin painted scenery and made program drawings. The
Théâtre d'Art became the first theater to produce Maeterlinck.
Other writers for the theater included Pierre Quillard, Charles
Morice, Remy de Gourmont, Jean-Napoléon Roinard, Charles van
Lerberghe, Catulle Mendès, and Rachilde. Among the ambitious
productions of supposedly "unplayable" works were Shelley's
The Cenci, a portion of the Iliad, and the "Song of Songs" from
the Bible.[19] After 1892, when the theater could no longer sustain
itself financially and Fort decided to concentrate on his own
poetry, Lugné-Poe shouldered the symbolist project and went on
to found the Théâtre de l'Oeuvre, where he produced Ibsen,
Strindberg, Björnson, and Alfred Jarry. But it was the Théâtre
d'Art that pioneered the symbolist experiment in theater. "What
had been inconceivable [onstage] in 1889 would no longer be so
by 1893."[20]

Rachilde contributed to this revolution in dramaturgy. On the
night of the Paul Fort's first *répétition générale* (final dress rehearsal,
open to a large invited audience), 18 November 1890, Rachilde's
play *La Voix du sang* (*Voice of Blood*) attracted a fashionable literary
crowd. Spectators came because of Rachilde's personal reputation,
not for the style of the play itself, which many reviewers recognized as belonging more to the naturalist theater than to the stage
of idealist innovation. The Salle Duprez was filled beyond its
capacity; ticket holders who arrived late found their seats occu-
pied. One reviewer noted the presence of the whole editorial staff
from the *Mercure de France,* "most of the Paris critics," and a vari-
ety of poets, painters, musicians, and writers.[21] *La Voix du sang*

appeared on a bill with two other plays, but it was the critics' favorite and was applauded at length.

Rachilde's ironic one-act shows a smug couple who drink tea to calm their digestion after a rich dinner. They complain about their maid's laziness, and they are pleased with the docile behavior of their grown son, who has already gone to bed. Suddenly they hear someone screaming "Murder!" in the street outside their apartment. The wife considers going outside to offer help, but the night is frosty, and they keep the curtains drawn. Just as they are about to retire, their son stumbles in and falls dead at their feet. The maid confesses that she was afraid to tell them that he had been secretly leaving the apartment late every night, probably to carouse in the cafés the elderly couple disdain. If there is a "voice of blood," the bourgeois couple has failed to hear it.

"This study has no other pretention than to paint one of the faults of Parisian egotism," wrote Edmond Stoulig. Willy (pseudonym of Henri Gauthier-Vilars, future husband of Colette) wrote that the "rapid scenario" was "ironic and macabre" enough to "disconcert" even Francisque Sarcey, an influential reviewer who was renowned for his opposition to newfangled theaters. Ernest Raynaud admired Rachilde's "virile" writing: "It is a play with cruel observation and studied construction, in spite of its apparent simplicity . . . This play is written in a virile way. It teems with wit, which will surprise no one, coming from Rachilde, a writer whose sharp, caustic talent people do not prize enough—however highly they may esteem it. It is true that Rachilde is a woman and we are molded with prejudices with regard to women . . . The characters are developed with skill and show that the author has scenic aptitudes of the first order."

Even if the playwright herself had "scenic aptitudes," *La Voix du sang* in production apparently missed the mark. Willy wrote that "the actor who plays the son is the only one whose diction can be praised without restriction (the role is a silent one, but don't say so)." Ernest Raynaud said that the actors performed "with conviction" and that the audience liked the "natural diction" of Lucie Dénac (as the wife), but he complained: "What a pity that this actress is of such a disproportionate size! When you saw her stand up from the armchair where she was embroidering, getting taller and taller, and spreading a black shadow over the little backdrop of the tiny set, the whole room almost burst out laughing!" Other visual gaffes bothered Raynaud. "It was the same when the maid entered, decked out in a headscarf of a most unbecoming yellow-mustard color." He added that "the son's entrance in no way produced the emotion you had a right to expect. You saw a gentleman in a black suit come out from behind the curtain at the back of the stage and come close to the footlights to execute a very cautious fall."

This actor's ineptitude was not the only problem that spoiled what ought to have been a *grand guignol* ending, leaving the audience gasping in shock and horror. Apparently there was no stage blood. Jules Renard's tongue-in-cheek review for the *Mercure* quoted conversations, like the following, which he claimed to have overheard in the audience: "Where's the blood? When you kill someone, doesn't it make blood?" "Monsieur, the whole world doesn't own a change of shirt." Was the Théâtre d'Art really too destitute to afford to spoil a couple of shirts with stage blood? It is possible. Paul Fort, when later asked how, as an impoverished poet, he had managed to pay his actors, answered that he had paid them "with their own enthusiasm . . . it was a time of youth and of faith."[22]

Renard's review caricatured Fort at the *répétition générale* as a person with no vision, trying to guess at a direction for his new theater. The literati in the hall congratulated themselves as if they

had written *La Voix du sang* themselves, said Renard, while the
public pretended to know what was going on and waited for a second act to explain things. He depicted their noticing how lifelike
the dialogue was: "It seems to me that these people talk like you
and me." "Like you, yes, but as for me, excuse me, I've been to
school!" Like Raynaud, they complained about the scarf and Mme
Dénac's height, and they (or Renard) found other bones to pick
with the production: "What's that on the mantel: a clock, a piggy-
bank, or a little bench under a checked handkerchief?" "I think
the murdered man is shouting too loudly." "True, someone being
murdered just has to shut up."

The invited audience at the *répétition générale* overlooked these
mishaps and warmly applauded the play, but the second night
audience greeted *La Voix du sang* coldly, according to Raynaud.
Willy gave Rachilde's risqué reputation as one possible explanation
for the audience response. He remembered "the cruel disappoint-
ment of several rather vicious friends . . . these gentlemen imagined that *La Voix du sang* could not help being awfully racy if written by the author of *Monsieur Vénus* and *La Marquise de Sade* . . .
Ah, Madame! You have deceived a lot of people!" Like Willy's
"vicious friends," Renard's imagined audience made snide remarks
about Rachilde: "A play by Mme Rachilde . . . will we have music,
at least? . . . To cover the words decently." Even though Willy
and Renard were Rachilde's friends, their coy tone about her supposed sensuality is typical of how most of her contemporaries
wrote about her.[23]

Like many of the reviewers, Renard recognized *La Voix du sang*
as a "bitter slice of life" in keeping with the naturalist Théâtre
Libre style, yet he called the style fresh and new: "This is it! A new
theater, no scenery, no tricks. Not a single aside. Never a false
exit." Eugène Cros called the play "theater without flim-flam or
artifice, real at last!" Georges Roussel thought the play "very well

acted, especially by Mme Dénac, with a simple, natural playing style of great truthfulness."

What are we to make of the enthusiasm of these reviewers for a realistic performance style at what was intended to be a poets' theater? It may seem odd that on the opening evening at the Théâtre d'Art, the most successful play was a thoroughly naturalist *quart d'heure*. But Fort's original impulse was to create an eclectic theater that would show the work of young people. Even though they might not have wanted to admit it, both symbolists and naturalists were part of an avant-garde whose common enemy was the commercial theater. It was only later that a symbolist style was discovered.

Even though *La Voix du sang* was more or less a *tranche de vie* (slice of life) and might well have appeared at the Théâtre Libre, the production began Paul Fort's close association with the writers at the *Mercure de France*. Rachilde joined the committee that chose plays for Fort's theater, and she tried to soften the blow for the stormy failure of his next production. In her review of *The Cenci* she called Fort "a hero" for even attempting Shelley's unwieldy, six-hour work. She took other reviewers to task for blaming the faults of the production on the performers instead of on a pedantic translation. Willy (future husband of Colette) had loudly complained about the "skinniness" of Georgette Camée in the leading role. Rachilde responded: "All women of great talent began by being skinny, O Willy!" and she went on to praise the young Camée for her "force of soul, suppleness, and ravishing grace." She ended her review with a comment on the good-looking legs of Prad, the lead actor.[24]

Rachilde and Willy's critical battleground was not the aesthetic style of the production, but the physical attractiveness of the performers. The controversy between the two reviewers reminds us that no matter how "cerebral" or "ideal" the symbolists intended a production to be, the libidinal effect of the actors on the audience could still make or break a show. To judge an actress by her looks, as Willy did, was more common in print than Rachilde's enthusiasm for Prad's legs. It must have seemed shocking for Rachilde even to admit noticing a man's limbs. Her comment may have been complicated by her "Mademoiselle Baudelaire" image and her desire to create a risqué impression in order to sell her own books. Her "real" personal response may have been something much tamer. Or she may have been trying to beat Willy at his own game: if Willy complained about Camée being too skinny, Rachilde could call her "ravishing" and also praise the lead actor's looks (in a way few other woman of her era would do).[25] According to Willy (and the aesthetic standards of his day) a thin woman just wasn't sexy. Rachilde associated thinness with young talent (or at least, for this review, she claimed that she did). Camée's later popularity with audiences as the premiere symbolist actress may have had as much to do with her sensual appeal as with the vocal technique and slow gestures for which she was acclaimed. The very reconstruction of a feminine erotic ideal—from round, soft, Rubenesque women to the wispy subjects of Pre-Raphaelite paintings—took place on stage, as well as on canvas and in society.

Camée played three major roles at the third program of the Théâtre d'Art (19–20 March 1891), including the title character in Rachilde's *Madame la Mort,* the central piece of the evening.[26] The author called the play a "cerebral drama," but the first and third acts were essentially realist. Rachilde's innovation was to try to show a subjective inner truth by locating the second act inside the protagonist's mind. In the first act, Paul Dartigny is a neurotic, bored, decadent "type" who despises ordinary existence and longs for death, whom he imagines as a beautiful woman. Paul evades the prosaic company of his mistress Lucie and his best friend Jacques, who has come to borrow money. The final scene of Act 1

shows Paul smoking a poisoned cigar in an effort to commit suicide. Act 2 takes place in a mysterious garden where two women
struggle for possession of Paul. The Lady Death of the title, veiled
in gray, defeats the incarnation of Life, played by Lucie in a fashionable evening gown. Act 3 returns to the realistic smoking room
as Jacques and Lucie discover Paul's body, arrange his possessions,
and console each other. The doctor who provided the poison
washes his hands.

The play's fusion of domestic drama, melodrama, and heavy-
handed allegory might seem tiresome today, but the second act's
attempt to show the soul onstage fascinated many of Rachilde's
contemporaries. Of the twenty reviews of the production, only
two condemned the second act, although a few critics found fault
with how it was performed, and many thought that the other-
worldly garden scene made the following "realistic" act unneces-
sary. The audience responded with two curtain calls and repeated
applause, according to the reviewer from *L'Ermitage.* Even Otto
Brandès, a less partisan witness, wrote that the play met with
"completely extraordinary success" and that the audience called
out Rachilde's name "with frenzy."

Part of the enthusiasm can be ascribed to the special nature of
the audience. Rachilde had asked her friend Barrès to get some
publicity for the play into the mainstream *Figaro,* claiming that
she herself never saw "the more important journalists, or even
their *cooks.*" She wrote, "I know no one . . . or rather, don't want
to know anyone!"[27] This disingenuous assertion (clearly false,
given Rachilde's salon activity) makes sense as a statement of her
aesthetic intent. Despite the tumultuous opening night response
to her play, Rachilde wrote that on the second evening the fashionable columnists all arrived "completely entrenched in a terrible,
icy mood. What will result from their disposition? I don't give a
damn . . . I never wrote for them and I'm on a cloud they will

never attain, they would treat me like a *wild beast* all over again."[28]

Later, in a polemic defending Paul Fort and attacking the Théâtre Libre's naturalist style, Rachilde called the Théâtre d'Art a "Temple," which would have a special public of literati, fervent young people, and most of all, a family of initiates, where "women of easy virtue," financiers, and powerful critics would not penetrate: "Violent storms will shake this temple, of course; the closer one gets to the sky, the louder the thunder; but we will get through our outbursts as a family, we will establish the desired electric current necessary for intellectual fusion from writers to critics; we will pay less, we will explain more, and we will no longer have the very boring task of having to waste time behind a row of street-walking feathered hats."[29] The passage is a wonderful example of Rachilde's over-the-top, inflammatory prose. Her reference to the presence of prostitutes in the theater, which evidently disgusted her, had some basis in fact: theaters were notorious meeting places for prostitutes and their clients.[30] Rachilde's strong reaction suggests what a fine line she herself walked as she earned a reputation as a respectable writer and salon hostess, yet continued to get mileage from the "Mademoiselle Baudelaire" persona. As she shaped her image to fit the decadents' beliefs about women, Rachilde risked the censure of the ordinary citizens who had treated her like a "wild beast" because of her daring novels. It was no wonder she called for an audience of initiates. The crowd that cheered *Madame la Mort*'s opening night was a select group.

The spectators at symbolist plays toyed with a kind of theatricality, wore strange clothes, and performed for each other in a more flamboyant way offstage than the onstage style of the actors, who tried to seem ghostly and inhuman.[31] Several contemporary reviewers remarked on the colorfulness of the crowd that night. Brandès, nonplussed by all the excitement, thought they must be mostly students. Roinard considered himself a member of the

group of "young people" who had come from the Latin quarter and
Montmartre "to prove they could gather into an army, without
leaders." Henri de Ban wrote that "during the intermission, the
house was superbly lit." He took advantage of the brightness to
make a list of the prominent literary figures in the "beautiful room
full of artists."[32] Georges Roussel, the reviewer for *La Plume,*
wrote the most vivid description of the spectators: "decadentish-
instrumentish-Maeterlinckish-symbolist poets, painters, neo-
traditionalist, pointillist-impressionist or not pointillist! So many
revolutionary mops of hair! All those floppy felt hats, in colors
which strangely complement one another! You would have thought
you were at an opening of the *Indépendents,* at an anarchist meeting, or even at the literary underground evenings at *La Plume.*"[33]

Even though she was surrounded by supporters who must have
shared the "desired electric current," Rachilde used her program
notes to explain exactly what she wanted the audience to see in her
play. Aware of the problems the Théâtre d'Art had undergone with
The Cenci, Rachilde wrote that she did not mean her play to be
"unperformable," but that "the scantiness of the theater's resources
forces me to the most elementary explanations." She wrote: "The
first scenes of the drama unfold *somewhere in life;* but the second
act takes place entirely in a dream, *inside the mind of a dying man,*
and since these death throes are caused by a powerful poison,
verium [sic] *oleander,* I tried to render palpable certain hallucinations, namely: the battle between *Life* and *Death,* who fight for the
body and soul of the neurotic man, each using their best arguments. (It is understood that *Lucie* in this second act personifies
Life, and not a particular woman, Paul Dartigny's mistress.)"
Rachilde's program spelled out her intended hybrid of quasi real-
ism and symbolism, leaving little guesswork for the audience and
perhaps belaboring her point. Many of the critics quoted her
explanation in their reviews; they seemed to need her instructions.

Rachilde's description of her intentions for the set is especially helpful to theater historians, given the lack of photographs or even drawings of most symbolist plays. In the 1890s, as now, most reviews retold plots or described actors, but critics were maddeningly vague about specific production details. Rachilde wrote: "In saying: *cerebral drama,* I wanted to indicate that it concerns an action *which, strictly speaking,* has no locale . . . And if there is a setting called the *smoking room* or the *living room,* another called the *garden,* that is because it would be very difficult for everything to happen completely in the clouds. So I beg the spectators to let the setting count for almost nothing." To ask the audience to ignore the setting meshed with the value the symbolists placed on the inner versus the physical. But Rachilde may also have been trying to avert criticism of the Théâtre d'Art's "scanty resources." Perhaps, like many playwrights, she was simply dissatisfied with the set for her play. On the other hand, when she defines "cerebral drama" as without "locale" ("*milieu*"), she implies that the whole play, not just the second act, was supposed to seem outside the realm of terrestrial existence. Deak speculates that the smoking room set may have been minimal and that possibly the actors performed in front of a painted backdrop.[34]

Several contemporary critics found hidden meanings in the two "realistic" acts as well as in the garden scene. Brandès called the whole play "dramatized Schopenhauer." He wrote that "the absolute lack of moral sense which Lucie and Jacques oppose to *'Tis something better not to be,'* their affirmation of the *will to live* in the face of this total negation, functions with extraordinary power . . . This personification of the forces in man which affirm and deny existence, was not without a certain terrifying originality." The reviewer for *La Bataille* saw all the characters as allegorical figures, not just those in Act 2: Lucie represented Love, and Jacques, Friendship, the two highest forms of Life, which Rachilde undermined "with very subtle cruelty." Quillard described the realistic scenes in Acts 1 and 3 as if they were staged unrealistically:

> One evening, at least, the public was happy not to balk at the inadequacy of the scenery: it was while they listened and applauded, as was appropriate, to Rachilde's *Madame la Mort;* even though the play's characters were *modern* and perhaps one might have feared some discord, some bewilderment; but the characters existed, *by themselves,* outside of any era or any particular event, with such autonomy that no one noticed what a strange bourgeois dining room they were moving through: for everyone, the set represented the dark smoking room, draped in black, where Paul Dartigny died, so much did the sentences spoken make funeral veils float across his face, and thicken the mysterious, sacred shadow around him.[35]

Quillard's description can be read, as Deak does, as evidence for nonrealistic staging. But Quillard may also have been using Rachilde's play to argue for his pet idea, the primacy of language in drama; as he put it, *"language creates the scenery along with everything else."* Perhaps Quillard saw "funeral veils" which the rest of the audience did not.

In fact, a careful drawing of the ground plan for *Madame la Mort* exists, on a rare acting manuscript now in private hands in Paris. Penciled indications show where the actors were supposed to move. The smoking room apparently held pieces of solid furniture, placed in accordance with Rachilde's published stage directions, which read: "A very dark smoking room, draped in black. At left, in the back, a black sofa facing the audience. At right, a desk covered with papers, books, a cigar box, matches. At center, a small table covered with a black cloth, a small box on top of it. At the back, a double door. An enormous vase of mimosas on the mantel, at left, in front of a mirror. Armchairs and carpet, black with yellow brocade." The drawing of the *mise-en-scène* (or stage

set) on the front page of the manuscript shows exactly what
Rachilde describes. Each seat has a number. The manuscript of the
play itself, written in ink in Rachilde's handwriting, has been
folded several times. Probably it was carried in an actor's pocket
during rehearsals. Specific actors' movements are written in pencil
in someone else's handwriting, sometimes in words, sometimes in
numbers, which apparently correspond to numbers on the drawing. These penciled directions appear for all of the characters in
Act I. The pattern of actors' movements was not unusual or stylized; the evidence is that the actors performed Act I "as if in normal life."[36]

This apparently "normal" movement pattern does not prove
that the set was entirely realistic, of course. If Rachilde's stage
directions were followed, the black and yellow color scheme must
have accentuated the decadence of the protagonist. The prepon-
derance of black over yellow prefigures the victory of Death over
Life in the second act. And there may have been moments when a
sense of the beyond intruded upon the realistic smoking room. At
three places in the manuscript, the stage direction for "a pause"
("*Un temps*") is doubly underlined with red and blue ink. A fourth
"pause" has a three-sided box drawn around it in blue ink. These
inked-in lines may have served as simple reminders to actors not
to forget that they were supposed to be quiet for a moment, or
they may have given directions for unnaturally long silences.

Later performances of symbolist drama were noted for long,
drawn-out pauses; Maeterlinck theorized that in the spaces between
the words, the supernatural could enter. The length of the pauses
in Act I of *Madame la Mort* may possibly have been one of the earliest attempts to employ silence in a way that was to become a stan-
dard symbolist technique for approaching a dream state onstage.

But it was the second act that seemed innovative and dreamlike
to most contemporary reviewers, who variously described the gar-

Drawing of Madame La Mort by Paul Gauguin, commis-
sioned by Rachilde for the program of the original production. Courtesy Bibliothèque Nationale de France.

den scene as "the stuff of dreams"; "of remarkable dramatic movement and conciseness . . . a real coup, the loftiest thing the author
has ever written"; "like a poem by Edgard [*sic*] Poe . . . the strange
work of an artist." Even Georges Bonnamour, who thought the
play's attempted synthesis of styles pretentious, wrote that the second act brought "something original, curious, new, never seen
before, refreshing . . . if there had not been the first, boring act and
the third, nasty one, I would have applauded this attempt, encouraged the author, and hoped that in the future her efforts might
produce a better work."[37]

None of the reviewers described the physical setting for Act 2 in
any detail. Rachilde's printed stage direction reads: "The theater
shows a garden, on a spring day, in soft, hazy light. Banks of light-
colored shrubs and rose bushes. Dominating the stage in the back,
a cypress shrouded in gray mist. At center, a stone bench that
looks like a tomb." I found no drawing of the ground plan for this
act, nor any record of what artist painted the scenery, although
Willy's review refers to a garden in the style of Odilon Redon. The
manuscript's penciled indications for actors' movements are fewer
and less definite for the second act than for Act 1. To help with an
analysis of how the scene was performed, and to reach toward an
understanding of why the spectators found it so startlingly original, I turned to several sources: the text itself, the changes Rachilde
made from the manuscript to the published version, descriptions
by contemporary reviewers, Rachilde's memories of the production in a newspaper interview thirty years later, and the program
drawing by Paul Gauguin.

Clearly not a literal depiction of how Camée looked in the role
of the "veiled Woman," an analysis of the drawing may give a
sense of the intended mood for Act 2, since Rachilde commis-
sioned Gauguin's picture. For Brandès, who complained that the
one comprehensible part of the "hyper-original" program was the

train schedule on the back page, Gauguin's drawing showed "a huge question mark topped with a death's head, inside of which fits a ghostly, veiled figure: Madame la Mort." The drawing shows a languid, seemingly boneless form. To twentieth-century eyes, the figure looks chic and alluring rather than ghostly, although in 1891 her skinniness may have seemed asexual. What Brandès calls a "death's head" is an amorphous canopy which places the dot of the "question mark" above the figure instead of below. Her form-fitting dress seems to be part of her skin. She stretches out a fingerless hand (to be kissed, or to give a motherly caress?); her feet disappear into a cloud, which is curiously pointed in an angle that could be a pointed high heel—or a hoof, the foot of a devil-being. A close look at that angle gives a sense of relentless forward motion, the motion of a being whose feet cannot be seen. What Brandès sees as a bright "question mark" looks like a graceful boa, a body halo, and the dark inner corner of the halo intersects the woman's form just below the waist. There is thus a sense (intentional or not) of a black opening at the site of her pubic area, a suggestion that instead of being totally sheathed in her dress, she is open and penetrable.[38]

The Veiled Woman is the voice of power in *Madame la Mort,* yet she is also an absence. Lucie (Life) displays her low neckline, her long disheveled hair, and her diamonds, but the Woman's long gray shawl hides her whole body. The mystery is part of what attracts Paul. After she has blasted Lucie off the stage, he approaches the Woman as if in courtship, but her presence onstage infantilizes him. She becomes the master who gives stinging rebukes.

PAUL DARTIGNY: You will freeze my blood.
VEILED WOMAN: It is already frozen.
. . . .
PAUL DARTIGNY: I am impure: you will purify me.

VEILED WOMAN: By burning your bones.

. . . .

PAUL DARTIGNY: Must I be quiet?

VEILED WOMAN: You only imagine you speak.

He still pursues her with a sensual wish: "might I sometimes, sleepless in our shadowy bed, press your form against my chest, like the body of a woman . . . who would resist?" It is a fantasy, not of seduction, but of endless frustration, and of rape prevented by a man's subservience as well as by a woman's refusal. The Woman replies, like a voice from *Ecclesiastes,* that she represents the forgetfulness of "these vanities." She tells him, "You will sleep." He finally demands, "Can you tell me who you are, you, Death?" She answers, "in a very hollow voice," "I do not know." There may be nothing behind the veil. Rachilde herself seemed not to know who the Woman was. In the program, she disclaimed any responsibility for the Woman's words: "The personal ideas which I may have put into the mouth of the *Veiled Woman* have no value except as simple, necessary arguments for the course of the action."

Alfred Vallette wrote that in *Madame la Mort,* Death is "maternal."[39] He was particularly interested in the second act, but he thought that the lead actor, Paul Franck, should have used a special voice to keep the phantom quality necessary for the garden scene. In a later interview, Rachilde remembered that *"Madame la Mort* gave prominence to the actor who starred in it, but not to me . . . the good fellow played his role against the grain. I had conceived of an enigmatic, mysterious, disturbing hero; he played him 'big,' with huge gestures. He had an enormous success."[40] Willy wished that "the crackpot [Franck] would spare us his contortions, his huge eyes, all the baggage (sighs, wringing of hands, contorted mouth) of a young lead actor; I think his poignant immobility would have moved us." One wonders how Franck would have performed if Rachilde had accepted his offer to take morphine before playing the role![41]

In the manuscript version, Rachilde wrote a direction to the actors: "To help in the interpretation of this act—the characters who live in this garden being much more the forms of a dream than living creatures, the actors charged with these symbolic roles must speak with a less resonant voice than usual." She also wrote that the Veiled Woman should be played by a young, "supple" actress. Only Camée captured the voice and the ethereal presence Rachilde wanted, and her performance earned the praise of most critics. She had a "singular voice with the timing and cadences of music" (Lemonnier), a voice Roinard thought too "golden." She was "a very seductive Death" (Le Clerc). She was "sphinxlike" (De Ban), "strange and perverse in her primitive loveliness" (*Courrier*), and "very disturbing, under her layers of dust-colored veils, with which she covers the kneeling lover in a beautiful gesture" (*La Bataille*). Even Georges Bonnamour liked the "caressing Chants of the veiled lady, Death, but no doubt it makes sense to attribute their charm partly to the diction of Mlle Camée."[42]

In Rachilde's published version of *Madame la Mort* she made several changes to Act 2, particularly in the punctuation and in the stage directions. Where the manuscript ends sentences with periods or exclamation points, the published text has the characters end their sentences with dots, suggesting lengthened pauses (the sort of pause that critics would later call "Maeterlinckian," and still later, "Chekhovian"). Rachilde may have added the ellipses to increase a sense of otherworldliness, after she saw Franck's melodramatic misinterpretation of Act 2. But what prompted her changes to the stage directions for the Veiled Woman? Instead of just moving forward from the cypress at the rear of the stage, the Veiled Woman "advances slowly, slowly, and not as if walking: gliding." She moves "closer and closer" instead of the original "approaching," and the plain "advancing" becomes "gliding one step forward." In the published version, Rachilde spelled out more clearly the movement patterns of a being who was supposed to be "much more the form of a dream than a living creature." She also added character descriptions, the most complete of which is the section on the Veiled Woman. She became "a young, lithe woman, completely covered by a dust-gray veil over a long dress of the same gray. Mournful voice, but clear and sharp. She *never* shows her feet, nor her hands, nor her face: she is an apparition. She walks, turns, moves, without a sound, like a shadow, but gracefully. *She does not look like a ghost:* she is not returning from the dead, she has never existed. She is an image, not a living being."

Did Rachilde get her ideas for rewriting the directions for the Veiled Woman from the failures of the production, or from her observation of Camée's success in the role? Remembering the production more than thirty years after the fact, Rachilde said: "Why don't I do theater? Because I don't like it. Those rehearsals where you see everything you have pictured torn to shreds . . . no, I find that too distressing. You can't fulfill what the mind has imagined, in the theater . . . so, what good is it?"[43] But Rachilde's descriptions tended to stretch the truth. Camée was the first performer to use a "psalmodizing" style of speech that became the norm for symbolist productions.[44] Reviews of this and other plays indicate that she also found a slow, hypnotic style of movement. Camée's performance in *Madame la Mort* may have shown Rachilde (and the other symbolists) something they could not have "pictured" from the playtext alone, something they remained unwilling to admit: that the playwright's language could not "create the scenery along with everything else" without the creative involvement of the actor.

At times, the actors who performed in Rachilde's plays may have been more creative than the playwright might have liked.

L'Araignée de cristal (*The Crystal Spider*), the first French production at the Théâtre de l'Oeuvre, was performed in Paris in 1894
and taken on tour to Antwerp, Brussels, Copenhagen, Christiana,
and The Hague. A devouring, sensual mother, "resolved to meddle
in everything," goads her terror-stricken son into confessing his
fear of women and of mirrors—and eventually into getting his
throat cut by his mother's grand psyche-mirror (a standing mirror
on casters). Rachilde's text ends with the mother alone in the dark,
but when the production was on tour in Denmark, and perhaps
elsewhere as well, a more violent finale was substituted: the son,
played by Lugné-Poe, killed the mother, before running against
her mirror.[45] Whether Rachilde approved of this change, or even
knew about it, is unknown.

L'Araignée de cristal was published in the *Mercure de France* in
the early 1890s, along with several other plays, prose poems, and
stories by Rachilde, which she republished in *The Demon of the
Absurd* in 1894. Her contemporaries recognized that the collection
contained some of her finest and most carefully composed writing,
yet other than the *Araignée,* Lugné-Poe did not choose to produce
plays by Rachilde at his Théâtre de l'Oeuvre. Her *Le Vendeur de
soleil* (*The Sun Seller*) was produced by a rival symbolist theater,
the Théâtre de la Rive Gauche, in 1894. Rachilde had been working hard in support of Lugné, trying without success to get the
two theaters to merge. Perhaps the production of *Le Vendeur de
Soleil* had something to do with this effort.[46] Although Lugné
claimed to be in search of French plays for his theater, foreign
playwrights probably held more interest for him. On his theater's
stationery, the name "Henrik Ibsen" surrounded "Théâtre de
l'Oeuvre," and the Norwegian playwright inspired Lugné-Poe
more than any other writer, even though some critics thought that
Lugné's acting style was too "somnabulistic" to suit Ibsen's plays.

Volupté (*Pleasure*) shares the slow-motion, somnabulistic atmos-

phere the symbolists were trying to create, but at the same time it
is the most overtly sexual of Rachilde's dramas. Two adolescent
lovers sit in a forest clearing by a mysterious pool, where sparkling
green flies rustle and clouds now and then "cast strange watery
reflections" so that the daylight seems to disappear. The two
nameless characters are nervous. Afraid to talk directly about
"things we will never understand," the girl insists that they play a
sado-masochistic verbal game. She tells him what hurts her; he
tells her what gives him pleasure. His pleasures are aggressive and
painful: scraping his fingernail on glass, testing his nerve by nearly
cutting his finger with a razor, drinking wine to get a headache,
grabbing for a mouse that almost bites, putting her picture under
his pillow and imagining—but he is too embarrassed to tell her
about the "secret pleasures" at night in his bedroom.

She talks of passive, poeticized pain: feeling sorry for Christ,
letting drops of cold water roll down her neck, weeping for children who have no milk, playing a single high note on the piano
until her hand is "burning" and she nearly breaks into pieces. She
craves the touch of satin and imagines wearing a sheer blouse with
a heavy pearl against each breast. Her favorite pain is the scent of
hyacinths—lying on the ground with her face next to a hyacinth,
her skirt thrown over her head, breathing in all the fragrance,
which she says smells like her heart. "You will never know my
heart," she tells the boy; she thinks he is an insensitive brute, an
animal.

Her fiancé, impatient with her poetry, wants to unfasten her
blouse. Even though she is clearly aroused, "it wouldn't be proper"
to let him caress her breasts. The sparkling flies suddenly swarm
up. After a moment of silence, the two lovers furtively kiss, in
mutual fear. She allows him to touch her long blond hair, wet
from the pool, and she permits him to drink water from her hands
as she leans over the pool to look at herself, displacing her body

and her sexuality into the dark water. When he drinks her reflection he feels a moment of ecstatic release: "From now on I'll carry you everywhere." She disdains the offer to share his pleasure: "I won't drink out of a boy's hands." As she looks into the water she sees the corpse of a woman with an open mouth, the emblem of her own repressed guilt over sex. She faints, and her lover, finally terrified by the unknown, carries her away without looking into the pool.

Volupté appeared in the *Mercure de France* in 1893 and in *The Demon of the Absurd* in 1894. It was finally performed on 4 May 1896 at the Athenée-Comique, on a double bill with a longer symbolist play, *La Lépreuse* (*The Woman Leper*), as a benefit for the actress Louise France.[47] Rachilde wrote to her friend Catulle Mendès that the performance of *Volupté* would be far better than her original published version. Paul Franck, who played the boy, "completely revised" the play, she said. "It was stupid before he fixed it . . . you'll see."[48] The revised script is now lost, but reviewers wrote that the performance ended with violence, as in the Denmark production of the *Araignée*: the two lovers played at strangling each other, the boy killed the girl, and then he sobbed alone in despair. Jean de Tinan thought the original ending more "beautiful." He speculated that "these gentlemen" must have decided the play lacked action, and that even though action undermined "Dream," the stage adaptation was "logical and very scenic."[49] The lack of closure in the original conclusion prefigures an absurdist theater aesthetic. It also assigns more power to the girl, whose fantasies drive the plot and who orders the boy to carry her away "without looking at the water" in the final lines of the published play.

Critics friendly to the symbolists praised the play, but the mainstream press found it morbid and incomprehensible. The *Figaro* reviewer wrote: "I'll say just a word about Madame

Rachilde's one-act. A perverse fifteen-year-old boy and an hysteric of thirteen tell each other their pleasures. I imagine they don't tell everything: they say too much about it already . . . It's a case of hysteria without scientific interest, artistic emotion, or moral purpose."[50] Catulle Mendès said that the audience laughed in the wrong places from time to time, but responded with appropriate applause at the end. Even though he thought the play a bit "horrifying," he wrote that Rachilde's "gracefully subtle" images made *Volupté* "infinitely delicate, almost innocent." If the two children were unconscious heirs to the Marquis de Sade, he said, this was a de Sade who remembered that the Laura of the Petrarchan love sonnets had been in his family, "Laura de Sade, in fact."[51]

Camille Mauclair compared *Volupté*'s "demon" to Edgar Allan Poe's description of perversity and said that the play made the spectators shiver at the intervention of the strange into ordinary existence. Mauclair had already written an extravagant article in praise of the "lust" in Rachilde's novel *L'Animale,*[52] even though a close reading of her works shows repression and guilt rather than the sexual freedom Mauclair celebrated. In *Volupté,* he said, Rachilde had "invented a modern fear," without affectation or pomposity, in one of the most "interesting plays of the season."[53] G-L. Maurevert admired Rachilde's gifts as a writer, "so virile and so feminine at the same time," with the unmistakable "pawprint" of the author of *La Marquise de Sade.*[54] De Tinan listened for the subterranean meanings in the conversation between the boy and girl. He said that, in "our ancient children's souls," Rachilde had discovered the roots of sensuality, the true "mystery of our bodies." (He added that young people today would consider it a matter of the utmost pride to "love sensuality as intensely as they could.") De Tinan thought that the two adolescents were looking for "intermediary sensations, where Objects would seem to be alive in order to merge with the new emotions of the young, anxious flesh."

Paul Franck was "delicious" in his childishness and "marvelous"
as a tragedian, according to Maurevert. De Tinan wrote that the
actors had just enough sincerity to make the play viable. He
praised Fanny Zaessinger in her first major role; she performed
naturally, without timidity, in portraying a perversity as pure and
sweet as her short skirt: "she succeeded in not being in the least
theatrical." Paul Franck triumphed in the passages where the boy's
"exaltation had to submit to the girl's unruffled calm," the pretended calm of a Princess of the interior, "eyes wide open, hesitant, afraid of her own smiles." Mauclair, too, liked Zaessinger's
acting, which seemed to him professional, despite her inexperi-
ence; he wrote that grace, emotion, "the charm of a pretty face, a
sweet voice, and intelligent diction" were things that could not be
taught.

Maurevert forbore speaking well of Zaessinger, in order not to
trespass on a certain M. Raitif, who, "everyone knows, 'discovered'
her yesterday morning . . . oh well . . . " Mendès said that "Mlle
Fanny" was "prettily inexperienced, with so much cunning already
in her innocence, or, if you will, so much innocence in her cunning." The terms of his praise echo the way contemporaries wrote
about Rachilde herself after she published *Monsieur Vénus.* The
reaction to her mixture of apparent chastity and perverse sexual
knowledge helped propel Rachilde's career as a novelist, even while
it closed some minds to considering her a serious playwright.

At times Rachilde's risqué image backfired. After the performance of her first play, Rachilde complained in a personal letter
that she was "perpetually treated as a pornographer in a country
where not a single man of letters knows how to write chastely—
I'm fed up with making those gentlemen smirk in that knowing
way men have. Anyway I've been fed up with everything for a very
long time, I'm so used to insults that it doesn't matter anymore to
hear that I'm a madwoman, an hysteric, a wild animal, depraved, a

bad Frenchwoman, handsome, very ugly, and completely outside the law—all at the same time." She added that she was glad that at least she wasn't being mistaken for a *bas-bleu* (bluestocking).[55]

Although some critics have seen Rachilde as an early feminist, many of her plays from the 1890s identify with the misogyny of her symbolist peers. The name "Mademoiselle Baudelaire" was apt. Baudelaire wrote, "Woman cannot separate the soul from the body. She is simplistic, like the brute beasts. A satirist would say that she has nothing but a body."[56] Unlike Rachilde's other plays, *Le Rôdeur* (*The Prowler*) has no male characters, but it does show women in a state of weakness. Four women convince each other that a strange man has penetrated their house and they run out into the night in panic.

The play wavers between absurdity and terror. The country kitchen setting, the ordinary activity of sifting beans, and the colloquial speech of the three domestics would make the piece seem like a comedy, were it not for Madame's fears and the nightmarish atmosphere they create. From the beginning of the play, when Madame enters making "uncertain gestures," it is clear that she inhabits a different, more rarefied world from that of her maidservants. Like the son, Terror-stricken, in the *Araignée* and the Girl in *Volupté*, she gradually affects the other characters with her dread. She fears the highway outside, the walnut tree, and the state of living unprotected by a man.

Little Celestine, the youngest and most suggestible servant, is both attracted and repelled by Madame's notion of a male prowler inside the house. As all three servants scramble through the dark to close the possible entrances, Celestine says she saw "something hiding" under the walnut tree. She fumbles the latch of the big door and hides her mistake. The others think a man is pushing against the door; she says she feels an arm under her skirt. By now the servants are screaming in the corridor. Even Celestine thinks "dreamily" that "perhaps it's true that someone was pushing the door."

Madame, terrified but determined, takes a candle and leads the group to lock the third and final entrance, at the top of a rotten staircase. Old Angela warns that they "can't be safe except under the sky" if the prowler is already inside. Now, one by one, each servant whispers that she can hear someone breathing behind her. They run to the balcony, down the stairs, and outside. Madame pauses for a moment, "cold sweat running down her face," then plants the candle on the threshold and runs out after them. "And all these women, their arms up in the air, run to their chancy salvation, into a dark countryside, while, resembling a funeral light, the candle continues to burn on the gaping threshold of this abandoned house."

Le Rôdeur first appeared in the *Mercure de France* in 1893, and was republished in *Demon of the Absurd* in 1894, but unlike *L'Araignée de cristal* and *Volupté,* it went unproduced until well into the twentieth century, when it was finally performed at the Théâtre Fémina in 1928. Reviews for this production have been difficult to find, but a performance in Pittsburgh in 1994 showed that the play's slow build of terror puts *Le Rôdeur* in a class with some of the best symbolist pieces. The many doorways, and the suggestion that ordinary sounds and objects carry omens of doom, are particularly reminiscent of Maeterlinck's *L'Intruse* (*The Intruder*), although in Rachilde's play the characters fear sexual attack rather than the unseen invasive presence of death that stalks Maeterlinck's people. The failure of the symbolists to produce Rachilde's play is something of a mystery. Perhaps the lack of male roles made *Le Rôdeur* unattractive to leading actors such as Lugné-Poe and Paul Franck, who may have found an all-woman cast inconceivable. The play's apparent scenic requirements—several different rooms, corridors, and staircases—may have made it seem technically impracticable in the 1890s; the stage directions suggest a short story rather than a play.[57] The problem of women's vulnerability to (imagined) male aggression, so topical in our own time, may have struck Rachilde's contemporaries as silly or unimportant.

Rachilde wrote, "I am a creature gifted, like all women, with excessive neurosis, and if I am not a neurotic, since I carry myself very well, I can still sound like one, like all women."[58] Several of her later plays speak with a more personal voice, perhaps more clearly a woman's perspective, than the plays of the early symbolist period. Rachilde's life and writing have been studied mainly in connection with the 1890s, but her career as a playwright, novelist, literary critic, salon hostess, social commentator, and Paris celebrity lasted long after the fading of the symbolist movement. Details about her private life after the turn of the century are more diffi-cult to find than the colorful stories from her younger years. Her published memoirs revolve around her youth, as if she were nos-talgic for her past image as a boyish, enticing amazon of letters. Outside the topics of some of her outlandish novels, Rachilde's politics grew increasingly conservative as she aged. After the out-break of the First World War, says Melanie Hawthorne, the mood of her writing changed from "light-hearted playfulness to a dark cynicism."[59] *Dans les puits* (*In the Pit*, 1918) and *Face à la peur* (*Facing Fear*, 1942) describe Rachilde's personal experience of the two world wars and her sense of separation from humankind. She tried to bring her pet rats along for both flights out of Paris, and she felt more compassion for fleeing dogs and horses than for human refugees, even her own daughter.

Rachilde's feelings of isolation predated both wars, though. At a breakneck pace of writing she published nineteen books between 1884 and 1900, many of them spewed out in one-month spurts, and she critiqued novels in a column for the *Mercure,* often read-ing and commenting on as many as forty books a month. Then her momentum slowed. Between 1901 and 1912, she published only four books. There was a gap of nearly seven years between her gothic historical novel, *Le Meneur de louves* (*Leader of She-wolves*, 1905) and her next novel, *Son printemps* (*His Springtime*, 1912). Rachilde wrote to her friend Aurel (pseudonym of Mme Alfred Mortier) that she hated staring at blank pages day after day.

Rachilde also complained of loneliness during the early part of the new century. Her close friend Alfred Jarry died in 1907.[60] Neither she nor her husband had much interest in raising their daughter Gabrielle, who was ignored by her parents in a reenactment of Rachilde's own solitary upbringing. (In fact, Rachilde asked, in *Dans les puits*, if pregnant women ever forgave their husbands, their "executioners.") Her marriage to Vallette was not unhappy, but he spent all his time at his desk, went to bed early, and refused to accompany his wife to parties and plays. Even though she had begun her career in Paris as a solo "reporter," somehow during the early years of her marriage Rachilde couldn't summon the nerve to venture out alone. She still presided over her Tuesday afternoon salon, where she was renowned for her loud laugh and her larger-than-life mannerisms, but she told Aurel that behind this façade, she felt numb. Claude Dauphiné believes that Rachilde suffered from severe moodswings and that today she would be diagnosed as a manic-depressive.[61] Rachilde's uneven patterns of writing—the years when she was churning out books and the other times when she felt blocked—may support this interpretation.

Rachilde didn't publicly admit to depression until she published *Dans les puits* after the First World War. By then she was revered as an important French literary figure and a lovably eccentric personality. A generation of young novelists depended on her erratic literary criticism for initial recognition. She wore mauve, her favorite color, and sported close-fitting velvet hats that hid her gray hair. During the 1920s she began to socialize at night without her husband, often escorted by handsome young men half her age. A contemporary noted that her penchant for "homosexuals" and "hairdressers" helped dispel gossip of adultery, despite the salacious titles of her novels.[62] French newspaper columnists regularly interviewed Rachilde on questions about sex, homosexuality, free love, nudity, and de Sade, to which she usually responded with witty remarks. But at the same time, she was losing her popularity as a writer, and the changing currents of artistic and cultural fashion were leaving her behind.

Although it is often difficult to read Rachilde's "real" feelings behind her many masks, her misanthropy was not a symbolist pose, and it does seem to have deepened after the First World War. Her loneliness may help explain the revulsion from life expressed in much of her twentieth-century writing, including two of the plays in this anthology. The protagonists in *La Poupée transparente* (*The Transparent Doll*, 1919) and *La Femme peinte* (*The Painted Woman*, 1921) court insanity as the only reasonable response to a crazy world. The young wife in *La Poupée transparente*, alone in a somewhat bare room in an asylum, talks to her imaginary son as she arranges a shawl over the corner of the couch where she "sees" him asleep. Her monologue reveals that she is not allowed to have scissors, since she cuts up the curtains to make lace costumes for the baby, and that she wants blue slippers for him "to go to paradise."

A doctor arrives with a commission from her husband: to try to persuade her give up her fantasy and resume an ordinary marriage. The doctor says that she suffers from an "overvivid imagination, a *flight of fancy*," which has caused a rift with her husband Albert; it will be her own fault if Albert turns to other women, "deprived of the joys of conjugal life." Her husband is willing to accept her "obsessions," take her back, and have another child. Angry that the doctor has not brought the blue shoes, she harangues him about the reality of the dead child and says that even though she knows he was born dead, he still lives: "fed by my mind, the *cerebral . . . chord* was never severed . . . I can't find any better way to describe the strange connection between a mother and her child." A kind of "superstitious terror" begins to overcome the doctor, who can almost see the glimmer of the transparent doll when she throws the shawl back from the sofa. The woman's beauty and her evident intelligence attract him, but his "self-respect as a doctor" does not allow him to believe in her "chimera." Finally he leaves, convinced that "one cannot cure crazy people who know how to argue their case." She drifts further into reverie, unobstructed by prosaic realities. Her madness has won the day.

Even though Rachilde's relationship with her own daughter continued to be strained, her evocation of the maternal bond in *La Poupée transparente* moved contemporary spectators, as well as the actresses who performed the leading role. The play was first performed in early 1919 for a small audience at the *Mercure de France* salon, with Georges Saillard as the Doctor and Cecilia Vellini as the Woman. Later that year, Louise Lara wanted to produce the play at her own Théâtre d'Art et Action. Rachilde's connection to Lara dated back to the early days of the Théâtre de l'Oeuvre, when she had tried to persuade Lugné-Poe to cultivate Lara's budding talent (Lugné disparaged Lara's ability but was obliged to put her onstage anyway, because he couldn't afford many professional actors). Rachilde wrote an "homage" to Lara early in the century. Lara later toured the new Soviet state and wrote enthusiastically about the theatrical innovations there during the 1920s; in name, at least, her theater of Art and Action tried to fuse a proletarian ideology with modern stage trends.

When Vellini discovered the plans for Lara's professional staging of the *Poupée,* she wrote distraught letters to Rachilde. At least one of the letters was stained with tears. Vellini said that she had become one with the Woman, that the role had to go to her, and that she couldn't understand why Rachilde would consider giving it to another actress. What had she done wrong? Lara had difficulty persuading Rachilde to allow the play to be produced at all; Rachilde claimed it was "nothing but a toy," not worth a real performance. Lara had been advertising *La Poupée transparente* since the summer, and eventually Rachilde relented, on condition that Saillard and Vellini both perform the piece again. Both actors asked Rachilde to hear them read their parts before the production. Lara made sure Rachilde attended at least one rehearsal (one of the few pieces of evidence that Rachilde became involved with how any of her plays were actually performed). The production on the afternoon of 9 December 1919 was preceded by Maurice Raynal's lecture on "The Art of being an Imbecile" and a florid "Homage to Rachilde" by Lara. Lara's "Boulevard Tuesday afternoon" programs were part of a noncommercial venture whose aim was to show works by young authors as well as "to render solemn homage to well-known writers and artists, worthy of such veneration." Rachilde had become an elder stateswoman of letters.

La Poupée transparente received at least two subsequent productions. Vellini and Saillard performed it again on 26 November 1920 at the Théâtre Albert I. The play received top billing over four other short pieces in a program called "Friday art," a series whose selection committee included Maeterlinck, Paul Fort, Antoine, and Mme Jane Catulle Mendès. Armory's review praised the play and the actors: Vellini was "eloquent" in the part of the mother, and Saillard "showed his well-known expertise" in the "strange play . . . which seems like some of Maeterlinck's dramas" in its "metaphysical" yet "vigorous" style. In June 1921, the play was produced in Geneva, Switzerland, with a different cast. Thérèse Frachat-Régnier wrote Rachilde at length thanking her for the chance to play the Woman and asking for permission to per-

form *Madame la Mort* and *Vendeur de soleil* as well. (No evidence
exists that Rachilde ever allowed her to perform these plays in
Switzerland.) The reviewer for *Journal de Genève* thought Régnier
was "perfect" as the distraught mother, but disliked the dim lighting: "It was an evening of Chinese shadows. Doesn't the facial
expression of the performer add anything to the gesture and
voice?" The critic for *La Suisse* wrote that *La Poupée* was a conden-
sation of "all the art and genius of the admirable Rachilde."[63]

More of Rachilde's "art and genius" appear in *La Femme peinte*,
published in August 1921. The play was apparently never performed, but it may be Rachilde's most intriguing commentary on
violence in sexual relationships. Her only play to deal directly with
the great war, *La Femme peinte* anticipates ideas that she explored
further in a novel she wrote in 1922, *Le Grand saigneur* (literally,
The Great Bloodletter, with a pun on the word *seigneur*, or lord.) As
in *L'Araignée de cristal* and *Volupté,* a mirror forms an essential part
of the physical and metaphorical setting for the play. An officer
talks with his actress mistress in her bedroom while she puts on
make-up; for most of the play the audience cannot see her face.
He resists her desire to know him better, to "exchange identity
papers," since for him "the incognito in love" is the essence of
desire. He wants her to stop him from sleeping or dreaming and
to help him forget. She wonders who it is that she reminds him of;
she wants him, just once, to spend the night asleep next to her;
and she is jealous of his wife, whom he calls a "girl-flower, like
you, only in a different garden."

She is jealous, too, of his experiences in the war, "this mysterious nightmare which was forbidden to us Others, women." She
knows that he makes love to her more brutally when she paints
her face, since he takes sadistic pleasure in "the lips most varnished
with blood." He says that her make-up "continues a tradition as
ancient as the first tears forced out by the master, the *male* . . . and

whose traces he did not wish to see." She wonders why he picked her, *"as if you recognized me,"* and she tells him she has heard him cry out in guilt when he was dreaming. Finally, in a monologue during which he demands that she not look at him, he confesses his complicity in the execution of a prostitute, a wartime traitor whom he had loved. As he describes the appearance of the corpse, his mistress applies make-up with feverish gestures. When she turns around she appears in full light, her face painted to look exactly like the grotesque dead woman he remembers. He begs his lover's forgiveness. She gives it, for "all the crucified women," in the name of love, stronger than death.

The soldier's self-hatred in *La Femme peinte* is more believable than the power of his mistress's love. *Le Grand saigneur* focuses on a former officer, traumatized by the horror of the trenches, who carries his wartime taste for blood into sadistic sexual relationships. Even though she put on a façade of dynamic enthusiasm, Rachilde was increasingly unhappy and out of step with her times. She disliked the short skirts and the new dancing styles of the 1920s, but she had never enjoyed dancing, because she had always limped. She claimed to hate modern music as well, although she formed a friendship with the singer Yvette Guilbert. More important to Rachilde's livelihood as a writer was her inability to connect to new movements in literature. In the first serious study of her "poetic" prose, Noel Santon compared Rachilde to Rimbaud, Baudelaire, and Dostoyevsky and praised her as one of the precursors of "a vast modern intellectual disquiet."[64] Rachilde's relationship to modernism has received too little critical attention. If the symbolists were misognynist, at least they had been fascinated with Woman as the Other, and so had left room for Rachilde to perform the part of that Other. The new modernist movements, on the other hand, were inhospitable to women artists and writers. Melanie Hawthorne suggests that "surrealism was part of a larger

modern reaction to women that underlay the angst of modernism
and the rise of fascism."[65]

After the First World War, both Rachilde and Vallette ridiculed
the Dadaist movement. Vallette refused to publish what he saw as
rubbish in the *Mercure*. Rachilde encouraged F. T. Marinetti and
the futurist movement in a warm (if vague) exchange of letters,
but she believed that Dadaism and surrealism were Germanic in
origin, and the war made her even more hostile to Germans than
she had been as a child. Her xenophobia started a riot in 1925 at
a banquet held in honor of the symbolist poet Saint-Pol-Roux.
The guest of honor, Rachilde, and Lugné-Poe were among the few
elderly representatives of the symbolist movement in a room full
of younger writers and artists, including surrealist poets and
painters who admired Saint-Pol-Roux. Everything went smoothly
until Rachilde made the remark that no self-respecting French
woman would ever marry a German. The painter Max Ernst saw
this as a personal insult. Shouts of "Down with France!" and
"Hurray for Germany!" were heard by appalled passers by, as the
banqueters began to pelt each other with food and kick dishes
off the tables. Rachilde claimed that Ernst kicked her in the stomach during the melée. The police stopped the riot by arresting
her and many of the other disturbers of the peace.[66]

Rachilde no longer belonged to "the young generation" or to
the literary avant-garde. Even though she was on the edge of the
circle of women writers patronized by the lesbian expatriate American writer Natalie Clifford Barney, Rachilde lost potential support
from feminists when she published a pamphlet in 1928, "Pourquoi
je ne suis pas féministe" ("Why I Am Not a Feminist"). The book
shows Rachilde's dislike for women in general more than an opposition to feminism per se, but it furthered her isolation. Barney
wrote that "Rachilde claims to love no one."[67] She was still known
for crazy escapades and surprising energy, but especially after the

1930s, her life became darker. She helped the careers of younger
writers by coauthoring novels. On her own, she turned increasingly to writing memoirs. Her husband Vallette died suddenly at
his desk in 1935, when Rachilde was seventy-five. She had already
stopped receiving visitors at her salon, and now she was without
companionship and financial support. Her eyesight was failing,
and she had difficulty walking. She needed to write to survive, and
she continued to do so; but her poor health, the Second World
War, and the slow disappearance of her audience all disrupted her
life. She published her last novel in 1942, although she did go on
to publish some poetry and more memoirs. She continued to live
above the *Mercure de France* offices in an apartment without a tele-
phone, with her pet rats and the antique furniture from her family.
Her daughter Gabrielle visited regularly, but by the time Rachilde
died, after a fall, in 1953, she was virtually forgotten as a writer.

The translations in this anthology may help correct this oblivion. Rachilde's sexual politics and sardonic humor make her plays
more interesting and performable today than those of some of her
famous contemporaries. Where male symbolists were obsessed
with death, in Rachilde's work death fuses with the fearful thrill of
sexuality. Characters who seem to exist part way between the real
world and the beyond infect their companions with terror. Gender
issues within the plays are not so clear-cut as to make it easy to
define Rachilde's feminism or antifeminism. I believe that she was,
as she claimed, an antifeminist, but that her surface beliefs were
belied by her ambition and her drive for status, and that her sneers
at "*les bas-bleus*" came from a desire to secure her position in the
decadent milieu. In her writing, her concerns about gender and
power make it clear that she couldn't help being part of the debate
she pretended to mock.

Rachilde played a major role in the formation of the symbolist
theater, which prepared the way for Artaud, Grotowski, Ionesco,

Genet, Beckett, and today's avant-garde. She threw her prestige behind Paul Fort, helped choose plays, and wrote pieces for the Théâtre d'Art, which attracted important critics and a fashionable audience. She fought battles over stylistic innovation. The Théâtre de l'Oeuvre may have owed its very existence to Rachilde's encouragement of the director, Lugné-Poe. But in the process of helping the first art theaters in Europe, Rachilde seems to have ignored her personal ambition. Only three of her plays were produced at the theaters she championed. That she pushed for others' work to be performed and effaced her own plays from the project to which she was devoted makes a striking statement about women in the early avant-garde. It is possible that Rachilde simply earned a better living writing novels than she would have if she had focused her energy on the stage. But for most symbolists, a woman's usefulness in art was as a stimulus to male fantasy. After a burst of renown as a playwright, Rachilde seems to have chosen to personify some of those fantasies and to serve in the "typical" feminine role of icon and handmaiden to the symbolist theater.

NOTES

1. Parts of this introduction originally appeared in Frazer Lively, "Rachilde, the Actor's Spectre, and Symbolist Dramaturgy: The Staging of *Madame la Mort*," *Nineteenth-Century Theatre* 23:1 (Summer–Winter 1995).

2. Barbey d'Aurevilly made this remark, which Rachilde quoted for the rest of her life. See Claude Dauphiné, *Rachilde* (Paris: Mercure de France, 1991), 74. Except where noted, all translations from the French are my own. Emphases are those of the original authors.

3. See, for example, Jennifer Birkett, "La Marquise de Sade," in *The Sins of the Fathers: Decadence in France , 1870–1914* (London: Quartet, 1986); Melanie C. Hawthorne, "Monsieur Vénus: A Critique of Gender Roles," *Nineteenth-Century French Studies* 16 (1–2) (1987–1988): 162–179; Hawthorne, "The Social Construction of Sexuality in Three Novels by Rachilde," *Michigan Romance Studies* 9 (1989): 49–59; Dorothy Kelly, *Fictional Gardens: Role*

and Representation in Nineteenth-Century French Narrative (Lincoln: Nebraska University Press, 1989); Renée A. Kingcaid, *Neurosis and Narrative: the Decadent Short Fiction of Proust, Lorrain, and Rachilde* (Carbondale: Southern Illinois University Press, 1992); Maryline Lukacher, *Maternal Fictions: Stendhal, Sand, Rachilde, and Bataille* (Durham: Duke University Press, 1994); Will L. McLendon, "Rachilde: Fin-de-siècle Perspective on Perversities," *Modernity and Revolution in Late Nineteenth-Century France,* ed. Barbara T. Cooper and Mary Donaldson-Evans (London: Associated University Presses, 1992); Robert E. Ziegler, "Fantasies of Partial Selves in Rachilde's *Le Démon de l'absurde,*" *Nineteenth-Century French Studies* 19:1 (1990): 122–131.

4. Frantisek Deak, *Symbolist Theater: The Formation of an Avant-Garde* (Baltimore: Johns Hopkins University Press, 1993), 227–238, does a careful reconstruction of the events on the opening night of *Ubu roi* and makes clear how Rachilde falsified the description of them in her memoir of Jarry, *Alfred Jarry, le surmâle des lettres* (Paris: Bernard Grasset, 1928).

5. Rachilde, "Réponse à un enquête," MS. 1896 (Paris: Bibliothèque littéraire Jacques Doucet), 1.

6. "Réponse," 3.

7. Rachilde, *Quand j'étais jeune* (Paris: Mercure de France, 1947), 9.

8. "Réponse," 1.

9. Birkett, 360.

10. Jean Lorrain, "Mademoiselle Salamandre," *Dans l'oratoire* (Paris: C. Dalou, 1888), 204.

11. Romana Severini, personal interview, Paris, 26 July 1993.

12. Auriant, *Souvenirs sur Madame Rachilde* (Rheims: A l'Ecart, 1989), 62.

13. Auriant, 62. André David, *Rachilde, homme de lettres* (Paris: Nouvelle revue critique, 1924) 20. David presents the permission granted by the prefect of police as a statement of fact, but his book is based for the most part on Rachilde's version of the story. Auriant includes a copy of the police report.

14. Ernest Gaubert, *Rachilde* (Paris: Sansot, 1907), 17.

15. J. Carrère, *La Plume* VI (1894): 137; quoted and trans. by John Henderson, *The First Avant-garde* (London: Harrap, 1971), 25.

16. A. Ehrhard, *Henrik Ibsen et le théâtre contemporain* (Paris: Lecène & Oudin, 1892), 465, quoted and trans. by Henderson, 26.

17. Maurice Maeterlinck, quoted in Lucien Muhlfield, "Le Symbolisme dramatique," *La Revue d'art dramatique*, 15 May 1891, 202.

18. Paul Fort, *Mes mémoires: Toute la vie d'un poète, 1872–1944* (Paris: Flammarion, 1944), 10–11.

19. Roinard translated "Le Cantique des cantiques" ("The Song of Songs") for the Théâtre d'Art's most scenically ambitious production. An attempt was made to orchestrate vowels, music, scent, and colors, in accordance with the theories of René Ghil, and the notion of correspondences and synaesthesia. The result was a flop: the repetitive movements of the actors bored much of the audience, which burst out laughing when they saw poets spraying scents from the balconies, especially when the odors were too strong.

20. Jeremy Whistle, ed., *Deux pièces symbolistes* (Exeter: University of Exeter, 1976), vii. For a more complete account of the moribund state of the French nineteenth-century commercial theater and the waves of naturalist and idealist innovation, see Henderson. For a fuller explication of the sources of symbolist theater and an argument that it was not simply a reaction to existing styles, see Deak.

21. Rachilde published a dossier of press notices for *La Voix du sang* and *Madame la Mort* in her first collection of plays, *Théâtre* (Paris: Savine, 1891). Except where otherwise noted, all of my quotations from reviews for these two plays are from this source.

22. Fort, 41.

23. The prurience with which her contemporaries regarded Rachilde lasted past her lifetime. Mario Praz sensationalized symbolist literature in *The Romantic Agony,* trans. Angus Davidson (1933; London: Oxford University Press, 1951). Rachilde's reputation as nothing but a two-bit pornographer, which persisted until recently, owes much to Praz.

24. Rachilde, "Un Orage artistique," *Le Carillon,* 25 Jan. 1891.

25. Rachilde almost always wrote for effect, not because she necessarily believed what she was saying. It sold books when she made risqué comments in print.

26. The roles were the Young Girl in Quillard's *La Fille aux mains coupées* (Girl with Severed Hands), the Veiled Woman (Death) in Rachilde's *Madame la Mort,* and a mother who prostitutes herself in order to feed her family in Chirac's *Prostituée.* This last piece, which ended the program, was a naturalist playlet which gave rise to jeers and hoots. Camée and the other actors apparently played their roles with seriousness to the end, despite the uproar.

Theater historians have paid much attention to the interesting staging of Quillard's play, in which a gauze veil separated the audience from the actors, who performed in front of a stylized backdrop painted by Sérusier. At the time, though, *Girl with Severed Hands* served as a short curtain raiser before the longer *Madame la Mort,* which reviewers saw as the most important play of the evening.

27. Rachilde, letter 77 to Maurice Barrès (Bibliothèque National de France).

28. Rachilde, letter 80 to Barrès (Bibliothèque National de France).

29. Rachilde, *Théâtre,* 21–22. This impassioned preface was first published as "De la fondation d'un théâtre d'art," *Théâtre d'Art* 3 (May 1891). Final phrase trans. in Henderson, 102. Laurence Senelick suggests the translation "waste time" instead of Henderson's more colorful, but inaccurate, "go foetus-gobbling."

30. Frederick Hemmings, *The Theatre Industry in Nineteenth-Century France* (New York: Cambridge University Press, 1993), 79–80. Hemmings refers to the presence of prostitutes in the French theaters as a "nuisance" and a "problem." He does not attempt to describe the situation from the economic or personal point of view of the prostitutes themselves, unlike Tracy Davis's analysis of the connection between prostitutes and actresses in Victorian Britain in her *Actresses as Working Women* (London: Routledge, 1991), 78–86.

31. The originator of this idea is Frantisek Deak, who further explores the self-conscious art of personality in the symbolist audiences (248–263).

32. De Ban's review provides the only specific information I have found on the lighting for the evening. Evidently the house lights were down during the performance, but I have been unable to discover whether Act II was lit so as to make the garden scene seem more ghostlike, with the use of "mists," for example.

33. Georges Roussel, review, *La Plume* (1891) (dossier of clippings, Fonds Doucet, Paris).

34. Deak, 148.

35. Pierre Quillard, "De l'inutilité absolue de la mise-en-scène exacte," letter to *La Revue d'Art Dramatique* 22 (1891).

36. For a copy of the stage set drawing, see "Rachilde, the Actor's Spectre, and Symbolist Dramaturgy," 53.

37. Georges Bonnamour, "Théâtre d'Art," *La Revue Indépendente* 19 (54) (April 1891). A few months later, Bonnamour reviewed Rachilde's first published collection of plays and was less kind; he wrote, "the simplest things become solemnly stupid under her pen" ("Théâtre par Mme Rachilde," *La Revue Indépendente* 20 [57] [July 1891]). Perhaps, for Bonnamour, the second act had a power in performance that it lacked on the page.

38. Rachilde was not satisfied with this drawing, and she asked Gauguin to read her play more carefully before he made the illustration that she would

use as a frontispiece for her *Théâtre*. She called the new drawing "ravishing." The second rendition of Madame la Mort is a bodiless head; there is no sense that she can be penetrated. The head is square, with a strong jaw and a troubled expression. Wisps of hair fly away from the face as if the woman is moving quickly through the air. The style of the drawing resembles Blake. Interestingly, in Rachilde's book, the picture was placed sideways, not right side up. The placement makes the subject seem like a geometrical shape instead of a person's face.

39. Even though Vallette was Rachilde's husband, he reviewed the production carefully and critically. He disliked the "romanticism" of the poisoned cigar and thought that the first act lacked "conciseness." He found fault with all the actors except Camée. Suzanne Gay as Lucie/Life was good, he wrote, but he pointed out that "vehemence is hardly passion." He said that Albert Félix as Jacques exaggerated his facial expressions and that Paul Franck as Paul Dartigny played the first act well, but not the second.

40. Rachilde, interview, *Cri de Paris* (12 Oct. 1924). In fact, Franck's success was far from "enormous," and it was Camée who became prominent as the premier symbolist performer. Here is an example of Rachilde's tendency to distort the truth.

41. See Rachilde, *Théâtre*, 29.

42. Bonnamour, April 1891.

43. Rachilde, *Cri* interview.

44. See Deak, 171–172.

45. See "N.," "De franske skuespillere paa Tivoli," *Dagbladet* (5 Oct. 1894) for a description of the Copenhagen performance. The review praised Lugné-Poe's skill in stage diction but found the evening essentially fruitless. *The Crystal Spider* is one of Rachilde's most interesting symbolist plays, but it has appeared in English translation twice and is therefore not included in this collection. For further information on the production, see Frazer Lively's introduction in Katherine Kelly, ed., *Modern Drama by Women* (London: Routledge, 1996), 269–272. The play also appears translated by Daniel Gerrould in his *Doubles, Demons, and Dreamers* (New York: Performing Arts Journal Publications / Johns Hopkins University Press, 1985).

46. *Le Vendeur de soleil*, an extended monologue in which a beggar tries to con the insensitive populace of Paris into noticing (and paying for) a gorgeous sunset, was originally published in *Théâtre* (1891). The play had several productions, including a showing at the studio of the futurist Valentine de Saint-Point in 1912, a production directed by Georges Pitoëff in Saint Peters-

burg in 1913, and performances in other European cities before the 1894 Rive
Gauche production, according to one review. To the young idealists who were
part of the symbolist movement, *Le Vendeur de soleil* represented their own
artistic superiority to their elders, the middle-class philistines who were inca-
pable of perceiving beauty.

Also in 1894 came the production of Rachilde's *Les Fils d'Adam* (*Adam's
Sons*) by an amateur theater society. In this comedy, a young wife comes crying home to her family after she discovers her husband's adultery. Given the
task of reprimanding the erring husband, her father and brothers instead
bond with him in memory and anticipation of their own escapades. The play
fits the realistic style of the "digestive plays" about marital infidelity that glut-
ted the commercial theater of Rachilde's day, although it has a proto-feminist
point. It was never published; the manuscript is at the Bibliothèque littéraire
Jacques Doucet in Paris.

47. Louise France was later to create the role of Mère Ubu in Jarry's *Ubu
roi*. She was known as a gifted comic actress.

48. Rachilde, letter to Catulle Mendès (18 April 1896).

49. Jean de Tinan, "Volupté" (press unknown; among Rachilde's press
clippings at the Fonds Doucet).

50. Review, *Le Figaro*, 7 May 1896.

51. Catulle Mendès, *L'Art au théâtre* (Paris: Charpentier, 1897), 228–229
(first published as a review, in *Journal*, 7 May 1896). Rachilde had a youthful
crush on Mendès during the early 1880s. What happened between the two is
not clear, but shortly after the relationship ended Rachilde went into a period
of seclusion. (Perhaps she had a nervous breakdown; she later said that her
legs were paralyzed and that her mother had to nurse her back to health). She
wrote *Monsieur Vénus* later in the same year. Rachilde's letters to Mendès are
among her papers at the Fonds Doucet. Doubtless he was remembering the
gauche young girl when he wrote about "Laura de Sade." Mendès and
Rachilde maintained a friendship until his death.

52. Camille Mauclair, "Eloge de la luxure," *Mercure de France* 8 (41) (May
1893): 43–50. It was perhaps because of this article that Rachilde dedicated
Volupté to Mauclair.

53. Camille Mauclair, review, in dossier of clippings, Fonds Doucet.

54. G.-L Maurevert, "A la Comédie-Parisienne," *Le Grand Journal*, 7 May
1896.

55. Rachilde, letter to Fernand Vanderem, 6 May 1897.

56. Charles Baudelaire, *Oeuvres complètes* (Paris: Pléiade, 1951), 1199;

quoted in Jean Pierrot, *The Decadent Imagination*, trans. Derek Coltman (Chicago: University of Chicago Press, 1981), 124.

57. My production of *Le Rôdeur* in 1994 did not try to show the doors, corridors, and staircases realistically, and even the "beans" became balls of cotton, meaningless bits of work that the servants passed from hand to hand in a repeating circle. Such scenography may have been outside the realm of Lugné-Poe's imagination in 1893.

58. "Pourquoi je ne suis pas féministe" (Paris: Editions de France, 1928), 44.

59. Melanie Hawthorne, "Rachilde," in *French Women Writers,* ed. Eva Sartori and Dorothy Zimmerman (New York: Greenwood, 1991), 152.

60. The nature of Jarry's and Rachilde's relationship has received much speculation, particularly among Jarry scholars. Some assume that the two writers were lovers; see, for example, J. A. Cutshall's interesting article, "Excuses Madame Rachilde: The Failure of Alfred Jarry's Novels," *Forum for Modern Language Studies* 24 (4) (Oct. 1988): 359–374. It is clear from their correspondence that Jarry felt emotionally close to Rachilde, but the evidence of her own writing suggests such a resistance to intimacy that Cutshall's assumption is hard to believe. Jarry's illnesses and addictions probably reduced his ability to engage in sexual activity. Rachilde and Vallette shared the task of supporting Jarry financially and bailing him out of difficulties. She persuaded Lugné-Poe to produce Jarry's *Ubu roi,* and devoted a memoir to Jarry (*Le Surmâle,* 1928). The literary and personal influence Rachilde and Jarry had upon one another deserves further attention.

61. Dauphiné, 142. Rachilde's letters to Aurel are among the manuscripts at the Bibliothèque National de France.

62. Paul Léautaud, *Journal littéraire,* vol. 9, entry for 26 May 1933 (Paris: Mercure de France, 1960). Léautaud worked for the *Mercure de France* and had little respect for Rachilde, whom he called a "crazy old lady." He described her salon as "Rachilde's Guignol" or puppet theater. Rachilde laughed when he told her that her associates were all rascals. "Of course they are," she said. "They've read my books." She claimed that her escorts took her to seedy places where she could make observations that would help her writing.

63. Reviews, letters, advertisements, and programs for *La Poupée transparente* are collected in a dossier at the Fonds Doucet.

64. Noël Santon, *La Poésie de Rachilde* (Paris: Le Rouge et le noir, 1928), 16.

65. Melanie Hawthorne, "Rachilde," *Dictionary of Literary Biography: Nineteenth-Century French Fiction Writers: Naturalism and Beyond, 1860–1900* (Detroit: Bruccoli, Clark, Layman, 1992), 238.

66. Roger Shattuck gives a delightful description of this event in *The Banquet Years* (Freeport, N.Y.: Books for Libraries Press, 1972), 359–360. News articles show that the old lady was terrified by the physical violence at the banquet, despite her literary interest in sado-masochism.

67. Natalie Clifford Barney, *Aventures de l'esprit* (Paris: Le Rouge et le noir, 1929), 206.

The Transparent Doll

La Poupée transparente

First performance

9 December 1919

Théâtre d'Art et Action

Characters

THE WOMAN, twenty-five years old

THE DOCTOR, thirty years old

The setting

A partially empty room. At center, a sofa
with scattered toys, a small teddy bear, a
colorful balloon, lead soldiers. As the curtain rises, the Woman, dressed in black,
holds a thick, opaque white shawl. She
carefully covers a corner of the sofa, as if
placing a blanket over someone.

THE WOMAN *(With a heavy voice)*

There . . . now I don't see him anymore, because he is sleeping. When my eyes are tired, he closes his. We vanish from each other and I am afraid. You never know if his sleep is the beginning of the end. Oh, life would be so long without him! If he never woke up again! Not to look for him anymore! Not to watch for his return! *(Mechanically, she straightens the wrinkles in the shawl.)* My poor baby! Already three years old, and he still doesn't talk! He can barely move, he just sleeps next to me. Only his eyes are alive. His eyes, mirrors of my own, his eyes which make me whole, which reflect the light I gave to them. *(She sits on the sofa next to the white shawl and puts the toys near it, so that whoever is asleep can reach them when he wakes.)* He never plays, he doesn't know how. I have to play for him. Life would be very sad if he couldn't hear the sound of a human voice, laughing, joking, thinking out loud. How would he learn to pronounce words, when no one ever calls us? And if he doesn't hear me laugh, chatter, and play, he will end up crying . . . I'm sure he will. But what bothers me even more than our isolation is his silence. *(She strokes the teddy bear.)* And you should be growling, you should jump around like a real live animal. Nothing is better for a sick child than a pet who comforts him without asking for anything in return. But you are just a poor teddy bear and I should replace you with a dog who will bark, a real dog . . . *(She thinks for a moment, her head in her hands, then speaks quickly.)* I really hope they'll put new curtains on my window! Then I can make him another lace shirt, a delicate shirt, full of light, a bright shirt. But I don't have beautiful fabrics at my disposal, and if I tear up the curtains with my fingernails, it's because I don't have scissors to cut the cloth. It's not easy to cut, to fold, to put together all the pieces without a sewing box. The last little costume, a trimmed coat, it was nothing but a simple half-curtain, and still, I made it look so charming. And if I had ribbons, and a little silk . . . Oh, I want shoes, too, pretty blue shoes with silk bows, some . . . what do they call them . . . baby shoes, yes, baby shoes: a soft leather bracelet that goes around the ankle and looks so pretty, with a big pearl on top. *(She sighs.)* But what am I saying! He doesn't need shoes! He doesn't walk. *(She murmurs, almost humming.)* A bright shirt . . . shoes of silver and glass . . . pretty clothes, to go to paradise . . . *(Her shoulders sink, and little by little she lowers her head, as if she, too, is falling asleep.)*

THE DOCTOR *(Enters softly from a door behind the sofa, at the back of the room)*
Madame! . . . I am honored to meet you . . . Madame Albert Aumier, is it not?

THE WOMAN (*Raising her head abruptly*)

Who are you? What do you want from me?

THE DOCTOR (*Hesitant yet warm*)

Don't let my arrival frighten you, my dear lady. I didn't go to
the trouble to have myself announced, but I am a friend . . . a
friend of your husband's . . . and he sent me . . . I was just passing by, I know this house very well and have often had occasion
to chat with the director here, an excellent man, by the way.
You are well off here, aren't you! There is nothing better than
this beautiful garden to help you get over an illness . . . and the
food here is first class. Yes, Madame, I have been sent . . .

THE WOMAN (*Interrupting him with a joyful cry*)

The little blue shoes! . . . You brought them! . . . Oh, if my husband thought of the little shoes, I know that he can read my
heart and I am certain . . . that the three of us can live together.

THE DOCTOR (*Embarrassed, examining her with curiosity and
admiration*)

I must tell you, my dear lady, that, in fact, he didn't speak of
that. That is to say . . . he wishes above all for us to talk rather
intimately. I will report your news to him and find out about
everything that you might need, of course. Do I have your permission to sit down?

THE WOMAN (*Motioning him away from the sofa*)

Not there! . . . Don't talk so loudly, Monsieur . . . he just fell
asleep!

THE DOCTOR (*Looks around the room; his eyes stop at the white
shawl.*)

Who? . . .

THE WOMAN (*Quite calm*)

My son, Monsieur.

(A pause)

THE DOCTOR *(Finds a chair, puts his hat down, and sits opposite the sofa, shaking his head)*

My Lord, Madame, I believe, I hope . . . that we will both come to understand each other. A doctor is also a confessor, and, like all confessors, he can forgive. But in this case the punishment seems to me to be too hard, as my friend Albert Aumier explained to me. He can't come visit you often. Beyond that, he told me what kind of woman you were, a creature of exquisite tenderness and warmth and of rare beauty also, I would add, even though he didn't say anything about that. *(He smiles.)* I wasn't living in France at the time of your marriage, but I remember everything Albert wrote me about you, and I was sorry not to meet you right away. And now here I am. I come to you, faithful to my mission, ambassador from a husband . . . who adores you. Yes, Madame, you are meant to be happy and adored, in spite of your overvivid imagination, also known as a "flight of fancy." You are a woman endowed with remarkable intelligence, but you came under the spell of that flight, which drove an abyss between you and Albert, and, I dare say, made my friend's life very abnormal . . .

THE WOMAN *(With cold contempt)*

Express yourself more simply, I don't understand big words. I would have understood his intentions . . . if you . . . had brought me the little blue shoes.

THE DOCTOR *(Very uneasy)*

Madame, please! I would like to approach certain subjects as a last resort, because the way you deal with them, with no regard for the actual series of events, it would be difficult for me . . .

THE WOMAN *(Ironically)*

Begin at the end, then.

THE DOCTOR *(Forcing a laugh)*

Gladly. With women, perhaps that is the best way to make one-self understood. Monsieur Albert Aumier asked me to beg you, in the name of his love for you, a love that he has proven, to agree to resume your life together. You are in good health, physically, that's obvious, and you probably understand that it would be quite excusable for a man your husband's age, deprived of the joys of conjugal life to . . . distract himself from time to time, and, up to a point, you would be responsible for that. There is no question of divorce. First of all, the law doesn't allow it. You have been very ill because of one of those mishaps which happen so often among young married couples, your nerves are a little affected, all in all nothing serious. Now your husband appeals to your intelligence and your good sense, to your reason, my dear lady . . . In short, Albert wants to take you back and allow you a certain . . . *mental* freedom. Lord, everyone has habits and shortcomings, and an educated man is one who can more or less accept his wife's obsessions. Some obsessions are absolutely harmless. Nevertheless, in order to be completely sane, one must filter some fantasies through the sieve of reality. You know very well that if two people adore each other nothing can destroy their conjugal life.

THE WOMAN *(Coldly)*

Indeed Monsieur, life . . . conjugal life is capable of anything.

THE DOCTOR *(Confused)*

Have I expressed myself badly? If so, I beg your pardon. We doctors are always a bit brutal. Listen to me, my dear lady, love can easily mend things. If you were to have a child, *another* child . . .

THE WOMAN *(Furious)*

Oh! . . . You said, "a child, *another* child"! . . . Then he must not have told you everything, explained everything to you, a doctor, you, a confessor. You whom he sent to me, his friend, our friend. Oh! It is certainly a punishment I don't deserve, and if I must go back to living in the same . . . sensible way, I absolutely refuse, I assure you. Now it's your turn to listen to me, Monsieur. *(She puts her hand on his arm, and he shrinks from her as she looks him straight in the eye.)* No! . . . No! . . . *(She smiles.)* Don't be afraid. The *violent* patients are not kept on this side of the building . . . And if they took away my scissors, it was to keep me from making shirts for my . . . phantom. In order to fight against the reality which you so generously offer me in place of this phantom, all I have is the power, the unique power of my will, my maternal passion. *I have a son!* Monsieur! You seem unaware of this fact. My husband keeps it a secret from everyone he sends to preach reconciliation to me . . . *(She draws the doctor further away and speaks to him in a hollow voice which visibly affects him little by little.)* Let's move away from the sofa. If I become angry, I will raise my voice and I will wake him. Even if I enjoy doing that, it will perhaps hurt him, because being roused from his limbo and jolted out of nothingness would probably not be a very pleasant experience! Monsieur, his big eyes are full of such sadness! When they open and look at mine, and when we look at each other, our eyes are immediately attracted to the same cold ray of light, the same sparkle of shattering glass . . . Oh, for a long time, the windows of our two souls have been drawn to each other! It is horrible to watch him look at me without ever saying why he reproaches me, this tiny little three-year-old child! And I swear to you, doctor, I do everything I can to take care of him in a normal way. You don't have to remind me of the hideous truth, it's always there. I am not pretending I don't know it. Thank God, I am no longer bound by worldly burdens, social conventions, and the affectations of newlyweds. I have no duty other than remorse. Yes, I cradle him, I play with him. Yes, they hear me singing sometimes, and that makes me sound like a madwoman, but am I any crazier now than before, when I carried him around but didn't take care of him and pretended he didn't exist? Monsieur, do you know where life begins, at exactly what part of the body the first sadness is born? Answer me! Where did you get the right to say he doesn't exist anymore and he should be replaced? Who says we must erase one shadow with another? Should we not rather help the little shadow in question as if he brightened our hearts . . . for eternity? *(She thinks for a moment and then speaks again, very emotionally.)* I had bought him a little teddy bear, a very quiet one, so that he would learn to accept his own silence, and a bright balloon with warm colors so that he could watch his dreams fly higher and higher, and small lead soldiers—oh, not to teach him the art of destruction, but because I want him to be a cautious man who knows how to line the soldiers up to guard his house . . . I would also like to have a real puppy so that this child could taste the sweetness of loyalty. Wouldn't that be nice, Monsieur, a loving, pretty dog who would get used to our prison? And then, doctor, since my husband is now in the habit of doing me favors, please persuade him to send little blue shoes for the day when my happiness, our happiness, will stand up and walk in front of us. Think of it, doctor, the little child has only me to defend him! He exists only through me, and I dare confess this amazing experience to you, an educated man . . . my child lives, fed by my mind, the *cerebral . . . cord* was never severed . . . I can't find any better way to describe the strange connection between a mother and her child. *(Feverishly, she clasps the hands of the doctor, who looks at her with a sort of superstitious terror.)* Please, forgive my lack of respect for science, but, soon, when he rises from the dead, you will see him . . . and naturally I will show him to you, even if he is nothing more than a fleeting glimmer, the glimmer of a soul—*a transparent doll*—your eyes will see that glimmer. And together, we will find a way to bring him back to reality, the reality of everyday conjugal life which pursues me but does not tempt me. Another child! Monsieur, this boy here is the first-born, a love child. He was not born alive! They told you that! You believed it! But even if my husband rejected him, I have saved him forever from your empty human realities. They wanted to do away with him before he saw the light of day. Albert Aumier condemned him to nothingness because he found me more beautiful without a child. He refused to love his own son, he preferred me to him. I was jealous and pru-dent, I understood everything. There must be a religious doc-trine for mothers, which abolishes all the conventions of sci-ence and society. They tore the flesh from my flesh, but they couldn't tear away my child's soul. And it grew up all by itself. Even if my poor little boy, unbaptized and nameless, can't speak or walk, he still exists. He is there, living, luminous, miracu-lous, ghostly, a first-born whom I will love forever. So look at him and be brave enough to go tell my husband that the child he sacrificed, I brought back to life. He speaks through my voice, cries through my eyes; he has my whole heart . . . *(Sud-denly she lifts the white shawl from the sofa. There is nothing there. The doctor shrinks back as she stretches out her hand.)* Do you see him? . . .

THE DOCTOR *(Looking only at the woman and speaking despite himself)*

As clearly as I see you now . . . I am afraid!

(A pause)

THE WOMAN *(Calm again)*

Thank you . . . From now on I won't complain. By showing him to someone, I brought him back to the world.

THE DOCTOR *(Trying to hide his emotion)*

I beg you, Madame, don't make me . . . lie when I am fully aware of the truth! In your presence, I am nothing but a deeply troubled man.

THE WOMAN *(Seating herself on the sofa, her eyes fixed on the empty space)*

Oh, I know! Fiancés, husbands, friends, you are nothing but men, and the compulsion for absolute happiness never afflicts you. Go, Monsieur, I won't stop you. You will end up asking me to compromise, even now that you have been lifted for a moment to the realm of my dream. Good-bye, doctor! When you meet Albert Aumier, don't forget to tell him that, as the saying goes, *the mother and child are doing well.* You owe me this formal testimony, at least.

THE DOCTOR *(Voice full of passion, he approaches the woman.)*

And what if tomorrow I bring you those little blue shoes you want so much? Might I then hope that . . . the three of us could be together?

THE WOMAN *(Uneasy, looking back and forth between the sofa and the doctor, who leans toward her)*

Won't he ever wake up? He is so pale! He looks as if he is about to disappear! Am I going to lose him again? Monsieur, what are you suggesting . . .

THE DOCTOR *(Impatient)*

Nothing that a very unhappy woman could not accept. Obviously, your husband cannot understand you. All the better if this nightmare disappears from your memory. All of that should disappear in the face of reality. You are young, you are beautiful, . . . and you have a life to live . . .

THE WOMAN *(Kneeling in front of the sofa and clasping her hands)*
Oh, my sweet little phantom, oh my soul . . . how can I live without you?

THE DOCTOR *(Recoiling)*
You can still see him!

THE WOMAN *(Stands up and covers the corner of the sofa with the white shawl)*
When I am in great pain, I find him again, *he comes back.* My sadness makes him come alive right in front of my eyes. You! *(With contempt)* It is over. You will never reach him. You don't know how to imagine him.

THE DOCTOR *(Drily)*
Madame, believe me, I will not play this game any longer. My self-respect as a doctor does not allow it.

THE WOMAN *(Indifferent to him, she seems to shiver.)*
Little blue shoes! . . . Shoes of silver and glass! . . . A bright shirt! . . . Beautiful clothes to make his way to paradise!

THE DOCTOR *(Gets his hat and, halfway to the door, turns back)*
Well then, each to our profession . . . After all, *(He sighs)* I like that better. One cannot cure crazy people who know how to argue their case.

Voice of Blood

La Voix du sang

To Paul Fort, Director of the Théâtre d'Art

First performance

Wednesday, 10 November 1890

Théâtre d'Art

Characters

THE HUSBAND

THE WIFE

THE SON

THE MAID

THE CONCIERGE

The setting

The play takes place in Paris, in an apartment on the fourth floor of a building overlooking a peaceful street.

Scene One

A small middle-class living room, comfortably furnished. At right, a warm fireplace and a table holding a lamp with a tasteful shade, a piece of knitting, balls of wool, a newspaper. At left, in the shadows, a window with a muslin shade behind long curtains. Door at the back.

THE HUSBAND *(Seated at the corner of the fireplace, his legs stretched out, his hands resting on the arms of his chair)*

Ah! . . . I think my dinner will sit well tonight . . . What time is it now, little Henriette?

THE WIFE *(Seated at the other side of the fireplace. Looks at the clock.)*

It isn't ten o'clock yet, my friend. Don't celebrate so soon, wait until you finish digesting.

THE HUSBAND *(Serious)*

You are right. *(He picks up the newspaper and leafs through it. The* WIFE *takes up her knitting. A moment of silence.)*

THE WIFE

What's the news?

THE HUSBAND

Oh, not much . . . Nothing but fiction . . . Believe me, they don't put enough facts in the papers. They're all full of children's stories. It seems to me they don't look hard enough for things that would be of interest to the subscribers. Even though I may be retired, business affairs will always interest me, and I don't understand why *Figaro* doesn't print the story of a major bankruptcy from time to time . . . I couldn't care less about their novels and their trifles! That sort of trash will never cultivate the mind! . . . Young people read newspapers only in cafés, where there is too much noise to grasp the author's meaning. And old men, like me, don't care about love stories anymore . . . Henriette, what if we asked for a cup of tea?

THE WIFE *(Slyly)*

You thought you were out of danger a minute ago.

THE HUSBAND *(Putting the newspaper down)*

That proves the old proverb: you have to kill a bear before you sell the skin . . . Yes, I think the quail stew was too heavy for me.

THE WIFE *(Self-righteously)*

I warned you. You ate two helpings: you have no sense . . . Regular tea or lemon?

THE HUSBAND

I am afraid of the lemon because of nighttime sweats. How about you, my dear?

THE WIFE

I prefer regular tea. We'll make it ourselves. Very weak, all
right?

THE HUSBAND

Yes, in our lovely silver tea service, old girl?

THE WIFE *(Rings for the maid.)*

Marie will bring the kettle, and then I'll send her off to bed,
because she has been complaining for several days now about
not getting enough sleep.

THE HUSBAND *(Shrugging his shoulders)*

Don't servants complain about everything? You are just too
nice!

THE WIFE

I'm telling you, it's so hard to find what you want! I have had
that cook for three years and I am going to keep her, because
she knows our habits. She is old—it is safer not to have a
young one with our son in the house—and she is still healthy.

THE HUSBAND

But, yesterday wasn't she talking about a numbness in her legs?

THE WIFE

Oh! We still have some time . . . from now until her first
rheumatism. *(She gets up and goes to get cups and a silver tray
from the china cabinet.)*

THE HUSBAND *(Sinking deeper into his armchair)*

It's so pleasant. This fire soothes my soul. After I drink my tea,
I'll be the happiest of men . . . Admit that the stew was a little
heavy for you as well . . . come on . . . There was a hell of a lot
of pepper.

THE WIFE *(Smiling)*

I only had one helping . . .

THE HUSBAND

You call me a big glutton, when you are one yourself!

THE WIFE *(Indulgently)*

We don't have quail often, and I know your weakness.

(The MAID *enters from the back.)*

THE MAID

Madame?

THE WIFE *(In a slightly stiff tone of voice)*

Bring us the teapot and some boiling water.

THE HUSBAND *(Self-importantly)*

Please, make sure the water is boiling, because with the cold draft in the hallway . . .

THE WIFE

Yes, make sure the water is really boiling, Marie.

THE MAID *(Worried)*

Are you going to stay up late? *(She quickly corrects herself.)* I am not asking Madame to let me go to bed, but . . .

THE HUSBAND *(Jokingly)*

No, you just want to stay up late with us!

THE WIFE

You can go to bed if you want.

THE MAID

Thank you, Madame. *(She heads for the door.)* I hardly got any sleep last night. *(She goes out.)*

THE HUSBAND

What's the matter with her, she looks upset!

THE WIFE

She was probably sleeping in the kitchen.

THE HUSBAND

It's amazing how lazy these people are. Anyway, her work isn't that bad!

THE WIFE

Oh, the way they talk! . . . When I was a girl, at my mother's house, the maids polished their copper pots every Saturday, all night long, and none of them thought about complaining. And on top of that, they got paid less.

THE HUSBAND *(Nodding his head)*

Sometimes, they didn't get paid at all: they served out of loyalty.

THE WIFE

Today it's a different story: either they're sluts or they're thieves.

THE HUSBAND

Aha! . . . They praise progress, but I say progress is the opposite of civilization. *(A pause)* So what do you say, shall we surprise our son and invite him to join us?

THE WIFE

He wouldn't like that at all. And anyway, he claimed he had a headache tonight. He must be sleeping. I think that boy needs his sleep: he works too hard.

THE HUSBAND *(Thoughtfully)*

Ah! He is probably still at it. Have you noticed how preoccupied he seems lately? He keeps everything inside. He's not an extrovert like us, and we never know what's on his mind. *(Putting on a young voice)* "Yes, Papa," "No, Mama": you can't get anything else out of him.

THE WIFE

Young people's secrets are childish. They wouldn't interest old people, my friend.

THE HUSBAND *(Dreamily)*

Gaston will be eighteen soon . . . Do you think he doesn't have a girl friend yet? . . . Just between us, that would be a miracle. He must have one.

THE WIFE

I don't get involved in his love affairs, but if he takes after me . . . *(a pause)* he will act like a gentleman.

THE HUSBAND *(Ingenuously)*

And if he's like me, he will never fall madly in love.

(The MAID *comes in with the kettle and the tea.)*

THE MAID

The water is boiling, Madame.

THE WIFE *(Sharply)*

Watch out! You will spill it.

THE MAID *(Puts the kettle in front of the fireplace and the tea on the table.)*

I'll go get the sugar . . . You didn't ask for it.

THE WIFE *(Annoyed)*

Oh, why couldn't you have brought everything at the same time? Now the water will get cold. *(She puts the kettle closer to the fire.)*

THE HUSBAND

Shall we invite the boy?

THE MAID *(Almost at the door, she looks distressed. She stops and turns around.)*

Monsieur?

THE WIFE *(Very irritated)*

Monsieur was talking to me!

THE HUSBAND *(Insistent)*

Is there a light on in Monsieur Gaston's bedroom?

THE MAID *(Quickly, as if afraid)*

Oh! No, absolutely not, Monsieur . . . He is in bed . . . I heard him turn his key in the lock, as usual.

THE WIFE *(Calmly)*

Did you fill the woodbox by his fireplace, Marie?

THE MAID *(Quickly)*

Yes, Madame, I filled it . . . with the biggest logs I could find. *(She leaves.)*

THE HUSBAND *(Sighing)*

Let him sleep in peace, that night owl . . . *(He goes to the table, while his* WIFE *pours the water in the teapot.)* Very weak, very weak . . .

THE WIFE

Don't worry. I don't want us to stay up late.

(The MAID *comes back with the sugar dish and puts it on the table.)*

THE MAID

You don't need anything else?

THE WIFE *(Coldly)*

No!

(The MAID *leaves. A pause.)*

THE WIFE *(Stirring her cup)*

You know our Gaston. He has such a positive attitude. He is much more serious since he's been living with us: a dormitory is not the place for a young man from a good family . . . The boy thought it over: he said to himself that he would have more money in his pockets if he stayed with us, instead of wasting his time in cafés and other dreadful places . . . Now he economizes . . . He is saving up already! . . . He wants to buy furniture for a smoking room. I will give him the little store room, behind the office. We'll make an opening in the wall, and with

Chinese straw mats, a rug, a ceiling lamp, green silk curtains, I will organize everything for him . . . We must indulge them in some fantasies, in order to reward their good behavior.

THE HUSBAND

Old girl, you aren't hoping to keep him in your skirts forever, like a little Jesus?

THE WIFE *(In a decided voice)*

Why not? If he likes it here! . . . *(A moment of silence. She looks at the clock.)* How is that quail doing, Charles?

THE HUSBAND

It's passing, dear, it's passing!

THE WIFE

Another little cup?

THE HUSBAND

Thank you.

(Noise of loud voices in the street)

THE WIFE *(Calmly)*

Listen! Do you hear? They're fighting down there.

THE HUSBAND

Drunks . . . It's carnival time!

THE WIFE *(Listening)*

With this cold, there are not many drunks in our street, no one walks by here after ten o'clock . . . And it's amazing that we can hear them so loudly from the fourth floor.

THE HUSBAND *(Stretched out blissfully in his armchair)*

Yes, it's cold as the devil tonight.

THE WIFE *(Yawns.)*

Shall we go to bed?

(A pitiful VOICE, *very weak, shouts in the street: "Thief! Murder! Murder!" The husband and wife get up and look at each other. A moment of silence.)*

THE HUSBAND

Some filthy bums?

THE WIFE *(Somewhat curious)*

Maybe a crime . . .

THE HUSBAND

There is never a policeman around here!

(In the street, the VOICE, *weaker and weaker, starts up again: "Help! . . . Help! . . . ")*

THE WIFE *(Going to the window)*

That man is getting beaten up! You can really hear him scream!

THE HUSBAND *(With a learned air)*

A phenomenon due to the intensity of the cold.

THE WIFE

If it wasn't so freezing, I would open the window to see . . .

THE HUSBAND *(Quickly)*

Come on! Oh! Come on! To open the window because someone is shouting in a street! . . . Women and their confounded imaginations! . . . Luckily, the servants' quarters overlook the courtyard, otherwise all the maids would go outside to watch drunken brawls! . . . Come along. I'm tired!

THE WIFE *(Still listening, after a pause)*

I can't hear anything now.

THE HUSBAND *(Laughing)*

Now you are paying for your curiosity: you wanted drama, but you can't have it!

THE WIFE *(Stops listening, moves the table away from the fireplace, puts the lamp back, and pokes at the fire.)*

I am always afraid of sparks. Let me pour the rest of the water on the fire . . . Now it's put out.

(A moment of silence. The HUSBAND *walks up and down the room to stretch his legs while he rubs his hands. The* VOICE *wails again.)*

THE HUSBAND *(Shaking his head)*

That sounds like a real murder . . . Some sordid affair. *(With disgust)* It will be in the papers tomorrow, you'll see.

THE WIFE *(With a bit of compassion, naïvely)*

Still, if we wanted, in a building like ours, with over twenty-five tenants . . . if we all went out at once . . . we could protect someone who was being attacked . . .

THE HUSBAND *(Amused)*

You are priceless, with your notions! Can you see all the men from this building, marching out with a banner? It would be ridiculous . . . *(More seriously)* No, everyone for himself, my dear, this is a matter for the police . . . when they aren't deaf! Let's go to bed. I am falling asleep . . . And the tea was good . . .

(A heavy sound shakes the house.)

THE WIFE

Someone is shutting the front door . . . The concierge must have been curious . . . *(She listens.)*

THE HUSBAND *(Also listening)*

That would surprise me, because our concierge is a serious man who isn't amused by nonsense outside the door! *(He smiles at his own words.)*

THE WIFE

It's more likely a tenant coming back from the theater.

THE HUSBAND

Madame Sacquier or Monsieur Lévy . . . I'll bet it's Monsieur
Lévy and he will tell us news about the murder.

THE WIFE

Tomorrow I'll send Marie to get the gossip.

THE HUSBAND

If it's Madame Sacquier, it's useless to ask her. She is not part of
our world, you know . . . and I don't think much of that creature, always dressed up like an actress . . .

THE WIFE *(Goes to the window and lifts the muslin shade.)*
What a night! . . . It's freezing! . . . The starts are so bright . . .
Lord! It's good to be at home, on a night like this!

THE HUSBAND

Too bad for anyone out in the streets! *(He listens.)* No . . .
Nothing . . . It's over.

THE WIFE

I can't see. We should have opened the window and looked . . .
(She shivers.) Certainly! And catch pneumonia! . . . *(She looks at
the clock.)* It's almost midnight. We're really living it up tonight!

THE HUSBAND *(Amused)*
Without even leaving the house! . . . *(He laughs and rubs his
hands again.)*

THE WIFE

We'll only sleep better for it.

(The door at the back opens abruptly. The MAID *appears.)*

Scene Two

THE MAID *(Arms in the air, face twisted with terror, wide-open
eyes. She speaks desperately.)*
Oh, Madame! . . . Oh, Madame! . . . *(She turns to face the door,*

*then runs backwards to the center of the room, her arms still in the
air. She seems fascinated and at the same time horrified by what
she sees in the black hole behind the open door.)*

THE WIFE *(Running to her)*

>   What is it? Are you insane?

THE HUSBAND *(Stammering)*

>   What? . . . What is it? . . . You aren't in bed yet?

(Supported by the CONCIERGE, *the* SON *appears, in a black suit, his
hands pressed against his shirt. His blond head is tilted back, he is
very pale, and he keeps opening his mouth as if trying to breathe.
When he gets to the middle of the room, his arms fall, and his parents
see a large red spot on his shirt.)*

THE WIFE

>   Gaston! *(She runs to him.)*

THE HUSBAND *(Simultaneously)*

>   My son! *(Stunned, he doesn't move.)*

(While the WIFE *feverishly unbuttons his shirt, the* SON *moves his
lips as if about to speak. Then his head falls to his chest, and he lies
inert in the arms of the* CONCIERGE, *who puts him down on the
floor.)*

THE MAID *(Kneeling next to the corpse)*

>   Oh, Madame! What a disaster! . . . The poor boy! . . . He went
>   out every night, and I never dared to tell you! . . .

Pleasure

Volupté

To Camille Mauclair

First performance

4 May 1896

Théâtre de la Rive Gauche

Characters

SHE, fourteen years old

HE, fifteen years old

The setting

A spring morning. A clearing in a forest. In
the middle of a thick carpet of moss, a
large round pool, like an enormous moon
of water. Clouds go by from time to time,
casting strange watery reflections in the
peaceful pool, and then the daylight seems
to leave the earth while the shadow of the
trees hides the sky. Around the pool rustle
insects of different colors, sparkling green
flies, and very tiny blue butterflies with
black stripes. Exquisite scent of wild vio-
lets. The two lovers sit near the water. They
stare down at the moss, no longer daring to
look at each other. They are nervous.

SHE

    These are things we will never understand, because our parents
    won't tell us.

HE

    What is there to understand?

SHE

    You are an idiot! You're a man, you should know.

HE

    I'm still just . . . a boy.

SHE *(Impatiently)*

    Look, I can't stand your attitude!

HE *(Suddenly furious)*

    And I hate the way you talk!

(A pause)

SHE *(Dreamily)*

No! It is unnatural, everything that's happening to us. Just
lately, I was reading in my prayer book: "And Jesus, hanging his
head, gave up the ghost." My whole body trembled. Why did I
tremble like that? I don't know, but it almost gave me pleasure
to feel pain and be sorry for Christ. *(She turns toward her lover.)*
Can I tell you everything that has hurt me, ever since we met?
And you will tell me everything that gives you pleasure? That
will be our game today.

HE *(Sulky)*

All right.

SHE

I started, it's your turn.

HE *(Sighing)*

Sometimes I stand in front of my window thinking about you,
even though you don't deserve it, and then I want to grate my
nail along the glass, and just thinking about that makes my
mouth water. I have to grate my nail, it's stronger than I am, I
have to do it! Windows seduce my nails. *(He spits.)*

SHE

What you're telling me is what hurts you. I asked you to tell me
what gave you pleasure.

HE

No, it's really a pleasure! You yourself told me that you enjoy
feeling sorry for Christ!

SHE

Oh! And I have much lovelier pains! When I wash, I press the
sponge against my neck and let the drops fall softly. They roll

down slowly and give me loathsome little chills, then they end up burning me, and I fall back into an armchair, laughing hysterically! Oh, it's a horrible pain! I have never been able to stop doing it to myself . . .

HE

That's not very funny! In fact, I can tell you an even more delightful pleasure. I put my finger on a razor-blade and say to myself: "One! Two! Three! . . . Go!" Then I immediately pull away from the razor when I know it's about to cut me. I imagine my blood running along the ground, and my finger falling off, wriggling around like a red snake. Oh, if anyone saw me, they'd think I was brave. Besides, every time I do it, I cut my skin a little, just a little.

SHE

The other morning, I picked a lily in the garden, a lily full of dew. First I shook off the dew . . . because of the birds. And I filled it up with fresh milk. It sparkled! It sparkled! It was like white champagne, with a scent of hot flowers. But my lily broke, and the milk spilled on my dress. I had to start sobbing when I thought of the little children who don't have milk to drink.

HE *(Affectionately)*

Yes, that's good of you, it was a kind thought. *(Curious)* Why did you shake the dew off? Dew isn't dirty.

SHE *(With dignity)*

Would you want me to drink it when all the birds in the country have touched it?

HE *(Naïvely)*

And the milk? You drank it after a calf touched it, because calves drink milk from cows.

SHE *(Disdainfully)*

No! What an idiot you are! As if it were necessary to talk about calves right now.

HE *(Confused)*

I can't think of any other pleasures. That's it for this game.

SHE *(Imperiously)*

Try.

HE *(Making an effort)*

I really like wine. It makes my head ache, but I drink a whole glass anyway.

SHE

What a stupid thing to enjoy! Anyway, no one says you can't. As for me, when I eat too much, I don't think I look like an angel anymore, and so, if I lived alone, I would only eat sponge cake!

HE *(Thinking)*

Wait a minute. You go so fast! *(He yawns.)* Oh! I have one! The other day I found a mouse in my closet, I grabbed it by the tail to kill it but it tried to bite me, so I dropped it. I was very glad to let it go.

SHE *(Laughing)*

You stupid fool! To let a mouse bite you! You should have come and found my green-eyed cat. She loves mice! With a single blow of her paw, she takes the skin off their heads, and they run around in all directions with little ruby bonnets!

HE *(Quickly)*

And then! And then! Oh! I still have all sorts of beautiful pleasures . . . When I go to bed, I put your picture under my pillow, and as I go to sleep I call you "my little woman." And then! . . . *(He stops, embarrassed.)* No, definitely not, these are secret pleasures, and I'd rather not tell you . . . Some things are just for me.

SHE

Sometimes, I play my easiest waltz very quickly on the piano, as if I were spinning and the keyboard were turning around me. And a passage where there is a high note, I repeat for hours, I end up striking just one single chord, that one high note on and on, until my hand is burning. It's like the sound of shattering crystal, it is sharp, sharp, and this teaches me extraordinary things. It penetrates my ear like a spiral feather, a diamond plume, a velvet brush. The other night, if Mama had not come into the room, I would have fallen and broken into pieces . . . Oh, and there is the pain of satin. I run my hands along my satin bedspread, and . . . you understand, one has small desires, little abrasions at the tips of the fingers, so my whole body shivers, it hurts so much to touch the soft fabric. It's like you, grating your fingers on window panes! I can't stop myself! There is the pain of unripe currants that I eat in secret, they sting my tongue and it's awful . . . The pain of wanting to have a sheer blouse, and two big pearls would sit on each of my breasts . . . The pain of smelling hyacinths! Oh, that one, my dear, you cannot imagine how much pleasure it gives me! I go lie down on the ground up against a big pink hyacinth which sticks up at the back of the garden, near a hedge. It's in the shade, like we are here. I pull my skirt up over my head and I put my arms around the flower so that all the perfume is mine, and I breathe . . . I breathe. . . It's like eating honey while the bees fly by and brush my eyelids with their sugary wings! *(She is almost swooning.)* You can't understand any of this! But it is so delicious that it makes me forget you! . . .

HE *(Sucking on a twig which he has just absentmindedly broken)*
Thank you very much! That's a pretty ridiculous story!

SHE

Do you know what hyacinths smell like?

HE *(Ironically)*

I guess they smell like hyacinth.

SHE

No, they smell like my heart!

HE *(Irritated)*

So you have smelled your own heart!

SHE

Yes! I am sure that it is a perfume box full of bell-flowers.

HE *(Laughing)*

That's impossible! Can I see it?

SHE *(Sighing)*

Oh, no, you will never see it.

(A pause)

HE *(Throwing his twig into the water with an angry gesture)*

You are very unpleasant to me today. We have only these few hours to spend together, and you use them to irritate me! . . .

(The sparkling flies swarm up all at once from the calm surface of the water and buzz around the two adolescents.)

SHE *(With vivid interest)*

Look at the beautiful flies. They look like floating emeralds on fire.

HE *(Wanting to flatter her)*

Or the eyes of your cat!

SHE

They are all wet, they glisten like drops of green water! Catch one, will you?

HE

But what if it stings me!

SHE

You're right! Don't startle them.

(They move closer together, as if to defend themselves against a possible attack.)

HE

I don't think they are dangerous. *(A fly settles on the girl's cheek.)* Look! This one thinks you are a plant. *(Graciously)* I am sure it smelled your heart. Frrrrrr . . . there it goes! And it didn't dare hurt you! *(Moved, they look at each other, and furtively kiss.)* Let's make peace! I have no more pleasures to talk about.

SHE

And I have no more pains to tell you. *(At this moment, the brightness of the pool vanishes as the sky darkens.)* Let's play something else!

HE *(Taking her hands)*

Let me unfasten your blouse and smell your heart, I need to!

SHE *(Embarrassed)*

It wouldn't be proper.

(She backs away a little and plays with the water. It sounds like pearls.)

HE *(On his knees)*

I beg you! . . . *(She throws water in his face.)* I want to!

(She breaks out laughing and turns over on her back, her hair tumbling down into the water.)

SHE

No! No! Not that, but I will allow you to caress my braids.

HE *(Already touching her wet hair)*

Does it smell of hyacinth, too? Give it to me! Give me your
hands, your little shell hands! Give me your face, give me your
waist . . . Oh, give me everything, since I will never have your
heart. *(He dries her hair with his kisses.)*

SHE

You are insufferable!

HE *(Looking passionately at her)*

I am thirsty! Let me drink water from your hands. It's strange,
my lips are burning. *(She fills her hands with water and holds
them out to him. He drinks, overwhelmed.)* It's like honey, it's
like milk, it's like blood, it's like wine, it's like brandy. It
embalms and it intoxicates. Yes, your hands smell like hyacinth!
Oh! I am so happy! *(He gazes at her.)* Listen! I know how to
possess you whether you want it or not. You will lean over the
pool and look at yourself, then you will give me water from
your reflection. That way I will drink your portrait and you will
be inside me forever! *(Anxious)* Would that be proper enough
for you?

SHE *(Smiling)*

Yes, on condition that I look only at my face. *(She leans over the
water.)* I can't see myself very well! Oh! This water is deep! It
looks as if this pool goes to the bottom of the earth, it's so
black! Oh! I can see myself . . . I can see myself . . . Look! I am
letting my hair down, you can taste it now, and since I am very
blond, it will be just like honey!

HE *(Shyly)*

So when it's your turn, will you drink me, too?

SHE *(With disdain)*

I won't drink out of a boy's hands.

HE (*Leaning devotedly over her hands, which she has again filled with water*)

Oh! Thank you anyway. You are so sweet when you want to be! (*He sips the water and sits up proudly.*) From now on, I'll carry you everywhere.

(*The pool brightens little by little, the clouds pass, the flies begin to buzz again in the sun.*)

SHE

Was it good?

HE (*Intoxicated*)

Like communion wine!

(*He rolls around at her feet like a puppy.*)

SHE (*Thoughtfully*)

When our parents let us get married, we will have our summer house built here. It's not too far from town, and the baker will bring us fresh bread every day. Because I can't live without fresh bread.

HE (*Looking up at her from the ground, with adoration*)

Is it true you think I'm stupid?

SHE (*Looking into the water absentmindedly*)

Yes! Yes! . . . We will have a nice poultry yard, and we'll eat roast chicken every day, except Sunday. Only, you will have to kill the chickens, because I am afraid of blood.

HE

Do you really love me?

SHE (*More and more distracted, changing her position several times*)

We will go riding every morning, I'll have a gray riding habit . . . Look! What is that in the middle of the pool? . . . We'll have a maid who will know how to change the style of my dresses every week, I'll follow the fashions . . . Lord! What is that down there? It's dark, dark! It's coming up to the surface, making bubbles . . . *(She stands up.)*

HE   *(Still lying on his back)*
  I adore you!

SHE
  Get up! We have to go back . . . Lord, this water is so clear! It is so blue at this moment that it's as if the sky has fallen into the moss . . .

(She goes closer to the pool and then lets out a terrible scream, which sets off faraway echoes.)

HE   *(Jumping up)*
  What's the matter, my love?

SHE   *(Turning around, terrified)*
  Don't move, I forbid you!

(She takes a few unsteady steps, then falls into his arms.)

HE   *(In despair)*
  She is hurt! Lord! She is going to die! Help!

SHE   *(In a stifled voice)*
  It's nothing, my dear! Let's go! *(Her voice becomes weaker and weaker.)* Carry me away without looking in the water, without looking in the water . . . *(She faints.)*

(Obediently, he carries her away. She looks like a dead woman, her arms hanging down inert, while the sun throws light on the other dead woman, whose white teeth shine in her open mouth under the clear water.)

The Painted Woman

La Femme peinte

To Federico Beltran

First published in 1921

Characters

LISIA, a woman applying make-up, thirty
years old

PAUL DE SARDRES, an officer, thirty-five
years old

The setting

Evening. A bedroom. At left, an unmade
bed. At right, a chaise longue where PAUL
DE SARDRES lies, smoking cigarettes. In
the back, at center, more brightly lit than
the rest of the stage, LISIA sits in front of a
dressing table. She wears a robe, her hair
falls to her shoulders. Her back turned
toward the audience, she looks in the mirror in order to paint herself or put on
make-up. When she speaks, she does not
have to turn around, because she can see
her lover in the mirror.

PAUL

You are so irritating, my dear child, with your relentless notion
that we must . . . know each other better! You know that's
almost an insult to me? I am a French officer, decorated, Legion
of Honor, and that's not enough for you? I thought after the
victory, that would be enough for anyone! *(He laughs with visible effort.)* I . . . married well because I was a soldier. I cheated
on my wife when I wanted because I was a soldier. I should be
a success at everything because I am a soldier, and I even imagine that I like you *(hesitating)* because I am still a soldier. And I
think, after that hell, a soldier's hell, anything should be
allowed to me, even paradise with you. *(He smokes.)* Look,
Lisia, I don't demand any details of you; it's enough for me that
you are beautiful! It would be too complicated to exchange

identity papers! Why the devil do you torment yourself with
the past? In view of what future? Can't the present satisfy us?
Love, if it exists, isn't it just in the present? And now it's lasted
almost three months, this present! *(He laughs, more bitterly, and
stretches his arms.)* You aren't bored already? Lisia, those who
cannot enjoy the incognito in love, don't have the right to
desire. Remember that ever since the world has been . . .
worldly, a mask has been the best way to flavor pleasure! A
mask! A wolf's head! The top of the face and its nobility are
concealed. The lofty forehead, the bright eyes, the whole mind,
the gaze, rigorously hidden: a mask shelters the blushes of
shame or the glances of hatred, but the mouth is free to kiss or
to bite . . . without explanation. *(He gets up.)* Why do you
shrug your shoulders like that? Look, Lisia! Who am I? I am
your lover. A fine man, a gentleman, a bourgeois officer, with
good manners, without a stain of blood or dirt. *(He goes to her,
hesitating a little.)* You want to talk after we make love? Sensible
words after insane actions? *(He takes the woman's hair in his
hands and plays with it.)* It is so dark, this black night of your
hair which throws me into oblivion and keeps me from sleeping . . . from dreaming. *(He laughs.)*

LISIA   *(In a heavy voice)*

Sleep? Have you ever had the time to live a life with me that
was even remotely intimate, remotely normal? To give one of
your nights entirely to me, up until morning?

PAUL   *(Ironically)*

Up until morning? That's a strange wish from a lover! Actually
to sleep next to you would be impossible, my dear child. What
a little wife you are turning into!

LISIA

Then you are afraid . . . that someone will hear you dream?

PAUL *(Trembling and looking around as if frightened)*

Hear me dream? Now you are talking like my wife! No, don't
demand the vulgarity of shared sleep. An exchange of two fantasies is certainly preferable to an exchange of identity papers!
. . . but not the contact between two bodies afterwards. It's idi-
otic! . . . Come on, it's late, Lisia. Where are we eating tonight?
Please, get dressed. Midnight, a time for crime, a time for rest.
Until then, I can enjoy myself with you and I put myself at
your disposal: you choose where we go. Let's go find noise,
bright lights, violent movement. And after dinner, what? Theater? A concert? Dancing? I am ready for any compromise that
will make me forget, especially forget your reproaches, your
suspicions. What suspicions? *(Angrily)* I never killed anyone,
except your enemies, Lisia!

LISIA *(Slowly)*

Theater? A concert? Dancing? And naturally, dinner in a low-
cut dress, under the indifference of big, cruel lights. I am only
an actress and *I* don't have the right to do anything but perform. Oh! . . . Your wife, she . . .

PAUL *(Drily)*

I have asked you not to talk about her here. *(Sarcastically)* I
haven't hidden it from you that I don't love her, but I forbid
you to remember that. I love nothing except the possibility of
forgetfulness. And she has much less influence over this possibility than you do. I want to be free of all fetters at certain
times, absolutely free to live in peace! And we have had peace,
they say, for a few years now. But just because I was at war, can't
I make my own peace, for myself alone? *(He becomes animated.)*
Lisia? We will go our separate ways if that's the best way for us
not to fight.

LISIA *(Her voice trembling)*

Already! So be it . . . if I disturb your habits so much. But then why did you pick me and come straight to me, *as if you recognized me?*

PAUL

You do yourself wrong. *(He laughs.)* You are unique, at least on earth, and if you had a double, I wouldn't want to know her. The woman you like at first sight, is, in effect, the one you recognize as your own, the one who . . . possesses you. Come on, Lisia, don't moan like a wounded dove! I hate that. Fix your hair. *(Lisia puts her hair up into a twist, then lets it fall back down, with an air of fatigue.)* One could really say that you are trying to provoke me this evening! Lisia! *(More softly)* Lisia . . .

LISIA

Do you like my name?

PAUL

It's a pretty name for a flower, the feminine for lily . . . and it will wither like everything else.

LISIA

Would you prefer the other one? This is only an artificial flower, unfortunately, a stage name. My real name is Agatha.

PAUL *(Trying to smile)*

Agate, a name for a precious stone, harder and more cruel, since you threw it into my garden. Lisia or Agatha, must I retreat, leave you, be alone again in the depths of a night, colder than the night of your hair?

LISIA

You don't want to have dinner here, the two of us, just with me? My maid is a wonderful chef, although she doesn't often get the chance to show off, the poor woman! I am never hungry!

PAUL

No.

LISIA

You don't want to rest after that, try to go to sleep . . . peacefully like a child . . . a child I would cradle?

PAUL

No. I am not a child. I am not innocent. I am a man, a former . . . soldier. *(He walks furiously up and down the room.)* And I was beginning to forget! Please, be quiet! Oh! To taste the silence of a mouth is to drink water from a calm lake! To finally put down your burden of sorrow, next to a mirror that reflects back to you a relaxed face, changed, bathed in joy. Oh, women, girl-flowers, idols painted with gold . . . or with blood . . . how can we live without you? *(He clutches his temples.)*

LISIA *(Tenderly)*

My dear . . .

PAUL *(Breathing with difficulty)*

Be quiet! . . . You were saying . . . that my wife? . . . She, too, is a girl-flower, in a different garden, that's all, a plant whose roots are better known. But she is so far from the earth we walk on, so far from the muck people hide under clean clothes! She is blond and very simple, like a stalk of wheat. In two years, she gave me two sons, first a little red-haired poppy, bursting with health, then a frail cornflower whose eyes are melting into the sky. Perhaps he will go blind . . . because his father has seen terrifying things. He will not live. And I fled, I left. *(Suddenly lowering his voice.)* You don't know why I fled my home? *(Whispering)* It's because of the dog. Yes, a little white fox terrier who licks the children's hands but growls at me for no reason when I go home. He doesn't like my smell. *(Making a fist.)* I ought to kill him, crush him, accidentally, while closing a door. I don't dare. *(Terrified)* Promise me, Lisia, you don't have a dog? You'll never have one? Swear to me! Extraordinary thing . . . this dog appeared from nowhere. They picked him up in the street where he was crying, following all the women . . .

LISIA *(Feverishly)*

I will be your only slave . . . but, please, don't break my heart! Don't close the door! Don't leave me . . . even though for you there is no love more powerful than death!

PAUL *(Preoccupied)*

These are only empty words, there is nothing like real suffering. Nothing is stronger than death, don't you see that? Death completely changes things, and out of a creature who didn't exist except in a state of more or less acceptable perversity, death brutally, irreparably erects an idol . . . stained with blood and gold, to whom, perhaps, one must make human sacrifices, an artificial woman, transfigured by martyrdom, who will never forgive. I am not crazy, Lisia . . . but I am afraid I will be.

LISIA

My poor dear Paul! Love is an absolution granted to us by the dead . . . that is how we know it is stronger than death. I have never loved anyone except you.

PAUL *(Rudely)*

In how many bodies?

LISIA *(She stands up, arms outstretched, without turning around, and drops her head in despair.)*

And you still carry your cross to me after how many sensuous crucifixions, my knight, my soldier, my executioner! . . .

PAUL *(Kneeling behind her and kissing her robe)*

Oh! If confession did not epitomize the most dreadful deception of old religions, I would tell you everything . . . but would you understand? Can't you at least pretend—you are an actress after all—and lure me into the snare of your caresses, and . . . avenge *the other?* You claim you have heard me dreaming? What did I scream that is worth the trouble of your loving compassion?

LISIA *(Quickly)*

This, Monsieur Paul de Sardres, which I never forgot: "*Is silence the same as complicity, even when one is not guilty?*" And then, you added, arguing with an invisible enemy: "*No, I won't speak, I have nothing more to say.*" That's all I have kept from the brief hour of your sleep, the only hour of abandon you have ever entrusted to me. I thought you must have witnessed terrible things out there, in that mysterious nightmare which was forbidden to the rest of us, the women. I became accustomed to the scorn of your silence. Then love invaded me while it fled you. I am not the kind of woman whom one marries and to whom one owes respect, that's understood, but tell me, why should I be forbidden to cure you . . . *since I resemble her?*

PAUL *(Still kneeling, his head in his hands, with a heavy voice)*

How do you know? Don't turn around. Don't look at me. I forbid you. How did you guess? . . . that you resemble her?

LISIA *(With a little nervous laugh)*

It's not difficult. You are only interested in my faults! She must have been uglier than I am. I am obsessed with putting on as much make-up when I go out as I do for the stage, and you like that. You have told me often enough that I look like a dead woman, or a sick one, who hides her decomposing features by using the artifices of the Egyptian queens. One day, when I had lined my nostrils with red pencil, you loved me longer . . . perhaps a bit too much.

PAUL *(Standing back up)*

In fact, I almost . . . strangled you. Oh! We'll never know for what sadistic games face paints were invented, those absurdities of fashion as old as the earth, and all that they can unleash in the secret instincts of men! It is in good taste to disdain this vulgar embellishment of beauty on a courtesan's face, but the servants of love continue a tradition as ancient as the first tears forced out by the master, the *male* . . . and *whose traces he did not wish to see!* All women, more and more now, after the storm of the war, all of them—prostitutes, women of the world, actresses, young girls who leave home to chase after husbands— they all use and abuse make-up. It is frightful and delicious, since it is still the lips most varnished with blood that we like best. *(A pause)* I implore you, Lisia, let's go out! Noise, lights! And stupid gestures of general joy in order to escape our individual suffering. I want to get out of here.

LISIA *(Sitting back down, resigned)*
I will put on make-up then, to please you. It will take a long time, because my hands are shaking. While you wait, tell me . . . whatever you like. *(Very tenderly)* Tell me your sorrow, it doesn't matter how; tell me because I love you and I can't help myself, my sweet, my dear . . . *(She leans over the mirror of her dressing table and kisses her lover's reflection.)*

PAUL *(Moving away and clenching his fists, fighting his emotions)*
Is the truth less frightful naked or painted? What good does it do to torment oneself over a dream, a very bad dream, a sense of remorse about a crime one has not even committed? This all fell on my shoulders for no reason, like brushing accidentally against a poisonous insect. *(A pause)* Listen, but don't look at me, Lisia. It was over there, in the beginning, when things were happening so fast and everything was going wrong. We began to realize that the largest shells were coming from their side. Our own little cannons seemed like hissing cats against their

mastodons covering the earth with prehistoric catastrophes.
And we were losing men, we were melting like shadows under
the sun. Oh, that sun, shining on all that and making our
brains boil! Disorder annulled all discipline, and except for
anger—that is to say the courage which kept us alive and feverish—we thought of nothing else but dying in order to see no
more. We had a troop in a village on a green hill, round like a
bouquet, blossoming, at night, with sinister corollas of purple.
It came down from all corners of the sky, like hail, and while
we waited for orders, we had to squeeze into the church, often
climbing down among the crypts, where you had the feeling
you were already choosing your tomb. All the villagers left, one
by one, dragging their animals or being dragged by them. I
myself had tied an old sick man to his magnificent milk cow.
All the villagers . . . No. There remained, still hanging on, one
woman and her dog, a tiny fox terrier, barking and playing,
excited, the joy of the village! The woman had been a seam-
stress in Paris, people said. She was a pretty brunette with blue
eyes, very elegant, always wearing powder and make-up, and
she liked to laugh with the high-ranking officers. She lived at
the edge of the village, far away from the church, in a charming
little house, a sort of *château-galant,* bristling with modern bat-
tlements, its tower a crystal helmet. It was ridiculous and pleasant, so very innocent, full of tranquility, so perfectly outside the
firing zone that . . . I went there sometimes, like the others. We
would have an hour of happiness, and champagne would oblit-
erate our despair . . . and then what had to happen happened!
. . . One night of heavy shelling, we noticed lights inside the
crystal dome. Who was over there? Not us, the officers, but the
soldiers of the watch, the footsoldiers, and then, the little fox
ran out, into the middle of a field, all white, following his mistress who was flourishing a bright parasol. The brave compan-

ion of our wartime pleasures made herself much too visible for
our safety, if not for her own.

One morning, the commander of the troop, clearing his
throat and overcome by emotion, said to me: "My friend, that
lady over there is a spy. We have all the proof now. Who could
have thought it? Did you suspect anything, you, her first
lover?" "No, sir," I answered astonished, "she is . . . a wonderful
hostess and has excellent champagne. I know nothing more."

During the investigation, all the soldiers from the front lines
told crazy stories, some out of jealousy perhaps, as they never
had the chance to hunt this private game. When she was in the
military prison, she changed from being very agreeable to acting almost aggressively. She defended herself like a lioness who
has already seen the instruments of torture, and even antici-
pated the accusations. There was no time to examine everything in depth, but there was more proof against her than it
would have taken to shoot two traitors. She was found guilty.
And then, when they pronounced the sentence, she looked at
me, the same way she had looked, one by one, at all the others,
my comrades. I was her first lover! She looked at me . . . I could
say nothing, neither for nor against her, since I knew nothing
of her life. She fixed her eyes on mine, her eyes full of curses,
tearless, contemptuous, painfully enigmatic, as if to say:
"Remember. You, of all people, don't you remember?"

They took her by the arms into her garden . . . she who had
lain in our arms! . . . And that night, everyone could sleep in
peace. At dawn, the order came to evacuate the area, since it
was no longer safe.

I swear to you, Lisia, that I hardly slept during the retreat
which the death of that witch had caused. No, and when I was
discharged, I galloped to the little garden at the friendly, pretty

house, that deceptive house, still looking innocent and happy
with its crystal roof.

I knew they had not buried her. The enemy was about to
invade the area and we wanted to show them how we punish
their spies.

Oh! That summer morning when bees and sparkling, dazzling insects hummed around the flowers . . . she was there, a
big flower, bowed down by a storm of iron, tied to the trunk of
an acacia, in the soft shadow of its thick leaves. And her bare
throat looked pale, her naked arms were tied, her black hair fell
around her, stiff with the sweat of agony, or with evening dew
. . . Oh, the terrible beauty of that face, the cheeks painted with
blood from the death shot, with vivid rouge like peonies, and
those fixed eyes, her eyes of green glass, unmoving, with blue,
half-closed lids, as if the skeleton finger of death could not close
them, even in murdering them. Oh, those lips, brown from the
blood coughed up in her final death rattle, and on her chin, an
enormous fly, a fat fly, blue, the same color as her eyelids. A dirty
beast which thrives on filth, I felt as if it had bitten *me!*

. . . And the fox terrier, her favorite toy, very small, very thin,
his delicate paws trembling, buried his head under her dress,
crying like a lost child, since they had spared his life to let him
die of starvation at the feet of his mistress.

But, all this, it was good, it was just, it was what had to be
done, it was the logic of war. *(A pause)* And that is why we all
carry, at our core, in spite of our ghastly illusions, for different
reasons and yet always the same, a horror without precedent
which either throws us into confusion or will make us madmen
until the fifth generation.

(During the last part of Paul's speech, LISIA, *who has listened atten-
tively, puts on make-up with feverish gestures. At the final word, when*

he stops, his arms crossed, behind her, she turns around and appears in full light, her face painted according to the description her lover has just given. She looks exactly like a portrait of the dead woman, only more beautiful.)

PAUL *(Looks at her for a moment, terrified, then falls to her feet, weeping. He cries out.)*

Forgive me!

LISIA *(Passionately holding him)*

Paul, my dear love, we forgive you, all of us, the crucified women, because we have this power in the name of love and by the laws of love, stronger than death.

The Prowler

Le Rôdeur

First performance

23 February 1928

Théâtre Fémina

Characters

MADAME

OLD ANGELA

BIG MARTHA

LITTLE CELESTINE

The setting

An isolated house in the country. Night is falling. In a large, somber kitchen, three servants, OLD ANGELA, BIG MARTHA, and LITTLE CELESTINE, sift beans. Their mistress, MADAME, enters and approaches them with uncertain gestures.

OLD ANGELA *(Jokingly)*
Like to help us, Madame? Oh! *There's* work!

BIG MARTHA *(Shaking out the pile of beans and spreading them on the table)*
There! We got plenty to do till midnight, and a good worker would be a big help.

LITTLE CELESTINE *(Smelling the beans that she holds in her hand)*
If only the husks didn't smell of rat piss . . . but they come from the hay loft, and up there, those dirty beasts don't care at all! *(She laughs.)*

MADAME *(Doleful)*
Light the candle, my poor girls. You'll ruin your eyes over there!

LITTLE CELESTINE *(Hurrying up)*

Yes, I told you so. The days have become shorter. The beautiful dew of the night falls much earlier. *(She lights a long candle and puts it on the table.)*

MADAME *(Sitting in front of the fireplace, behind the servants)*

Would you go shut the large window-door in the dining room, Celestine?

LITTLE CELESTINE *(Surprised)*

But why, Madame? It's not nine o'clock yet.

MADAME *(Talking to herself)*

After all, we are women, all alone!

BIG MARTHA *(Stops sifting.)*

Anything the matter, Madame? You act funny . . .

OLD ANGELA *(Looking up and observing Madame)*

Was there something wrong with your dinner?

MADAME *(Shifting on her chair)*

Ah! Do you find me pale? No! No! It's nothing . . . It's probably the highway, it's so white, in the middle of these black fields, it's so long . . . I must have looked at it for a long time . . . I would have liked it better if our house weren't along a highway.

LITTLE CELESTINE

As far as the highway goes, it's got a beautiful weaving tail. There, that's the honest truth. *(She sits down.)*

OLD ANGELA

And if the robbers came one night, we would have the time to see them coming, for sure!

BIG MARTHA *(Sententiously)*

The robbers, these days, don't travel the big highways anymore, they take the small side roads.

LITTLE CELESTINE *(Laughing, but uncertain)*

Is it because Madame worries about prowlers that her face is all twisted?

MADAME *(Drily)*

You are an idiot! A forty-year-old woman is not afraid of anything. No! I just felt a cold shiver suddenly, between my shoulders . . .

OLD ANGELA

Must boil sage and drink a big cup with honey.

MADAME *(Standing up)*

It took me by surprise, while I was looking at the highway, down there, next to the big walnut tree, and it seemed to me . . .

LITTLE CELESTINE *(Inquisitively)*

What did it seem like to you, Madame?

MADAME

It is indeed necessary sometimes to have a man in the house.

BIG MARTHA *(Quickly)*

There! I always said that Madame should remarry . . . You can't live without a man, after all!

OLD ANGELA *(In tears)*

Oh, if our late husbands weren't dead . . . everything would be better.

LITTLE CELESTINE *(Bitterly)*

That's true! We would be more at our ease here, and perhaps Madame might wish to be so gracious as to make an effort, if only for our sakes!

MADAME *(Dreamily)*

Or a dog . . . A dog that would bark at night . . .

BIG MARTHA *(Grumbling)*

But Madame says that they eat more than they are worth!

MADAME *(Shuddering)*

No, not a dog, barking at night . . . it would be terrible! *(She looks all around the kitchen.)* But anyway, the four of us, what would we do against a prowler?

LITTLE CELESTINE

Seems like there was a bad man at Claudin's house. He came in through the hay loft, went down during the night, when they were asleep, found an open door, and . . .

MADAME

Did he hurt anyone?

LITTLE CELESTINE

No!

MADAME

Did he make any noise?

LITTLE CELESTINE

No! He took off his shoes.

MADAME *(Very nervous)*

Then nobody saw him or heard him?

LITTLE CELESTINE *(With conviction)*

Nobody.

(A moment's silence)

OLD ANGELA *(With a hollow voice)*

I myself met a bad man once. I had gone to get water from the well, all the way to the end of the village. So while I was pulling, I felt the bucket heavy, heavy . . . there was a man in it. He hid there to scare me . . . and when I pulled him up, he said to me . . .

MADAME *(Interrupting her)*

Listen! It's all nonsense. There are three of you and there are three doors to shut in this house. Each of you run and shut one. What if it's not nine o'clock yet . . . We are not expecting anyone this evening . . . *(She walks up and down feverishly.)* The large window-door in the dining room shuts firmly . . . The entrance door along the corridor has a big metal padlock . . . And then, up there, the balcony door is well bolted . . . A prowler couldn't knock down all three doors. *(Turning toward the servants.)* Go ahead, move quickly . . .

BIG MARTHA *(In a bad mood)*

Thank you very much, I am not going alone. Someone's got to push the door leaf while I lock.

(All three throw their beans on the table.)

LITTLE CELESTINE *(Shivering)*

You know, it's true that it is sort of cold outside already.

MADAME

You really are cowards! Then go all together, but move quickly and don't forget to look around the walnut tree. I'll be waiting for you here.

(They light a lantern and exit.)

BIG MARTHA *(Speaking louder as she enters the dining room)*

Oh no! It's so dark in this dirty shack of a house!

OLD ANGELA *(Raising the lantern with shaky hands)*

We must look, alright. But me, I am not going out there.

LITTLE CELESTINE *(Leaning out of the large window-door)*

Well, here I go, so what? The walnut tree is still there.

BIG MARTHA *(Closing the shutters quickly)*

Good! Don't talk so loud. Trees are cunning.

(They return to the kitchen in a haste and push each other in order to come in first.)

LITTLE CELESTINE *(Feverishly)*

I looked Madame, I went out, I saw nothing, he can't come in, it's shut.

MADAME *(Worried)*

>   What *he?*

OLD ANGELA

>   But the prowler that Madame was talking about!

MADAME *(Exasperated)*

>   And the door in the corridor? And the balcony door?

BIG MARTHA

>   We're going! We're going! Let us breathe. *(She wipes her face with her apron.)*

MADAME *(To Celestine)*

>   So, you didn't see anything, did you?

LITTLE CELESTINE *(Out of breath)*

>   No . . . I mean yes, I saw the walnut tree . . .

MADAME *(Anxious)*

>   And then?

LITTLE CELESTINE

>   And then . . . In any event, I think I saw something, like something hiding.

MADAME *(Triumphant)*

>   There, you hear! Like something hiding! . . . I too, I think I saw that. Surely, the prowler who would want to enter our home would not start by showing himself . . .

THE THREE SERVANTS *(Together)*

>   Surely!

MADAME *(With authority)*

>   Let's move, hurry! The other two doors! We must not give him the time to penetrate, because then we'll lock him inside here.

(The three servants move quickly across from the dining room toward a very long corridor, and suddenly Little Celestine shouts out loud.)

OLD ANGELA

What now! Holy Virgin! Is this our last day on earth?

BIG MARTHA *(Pointing at Celestine, who has fallen on the floor)*

Are you done with playing silly?

LITTLE CELESTINE *(Bewitched)*

I walked on a toad . . . yes . . . I felt it alright . . . It was soft!
. . . *(She cries.)*

OLD ANGELA *(Searching with the lantern)*

It's not a toad, it's a bean husk . . . *(She grumbles.)* An unnatural
story, all the same!

*(All three run towards the door. Little Celestine gropes for the metal
bar. Big Martha pushes the door leaf. Old Angela, very troubled, lifts
the lantern in the wrong direction. No one can see anything.)*

BIG MARTHA

Who is pushing from the outside?

LITTLE CELESTINE

Oh Lord, I feel an arm reaching up my skirt.

BIG MARTHA *(Screaming)*

Madame! Madame! Someone is pushing the door! *(To Old
Angela)* Shine some light, you old owl!

*(Old Angela turns the lantern towards the door. Little Celestine real-
izes that she has put the metal bar between the two door leaves, so she
has made it impossible for the women to close the door. She pulls out
the bar without daring explain anything to anyone.)*

BIG MARTHA *(Breathlessly)*

There, that's it! . . . *(She locks the door.)* It's true, there was
someone . . .

*(They rush back into the kitchen, then fall into their chairs and grow
pale.)*

MADAME *(Exhausted)*

Why do you scream? It's frightful to hear you scream like that in the corridor! I'll go with you to the balcony door. I don't want to leave you alone anymore.

LITTLE CELESTINE *(Dreamily)*

Perhaps it's true that someone was pushing the door . . .

BIG MARTHA

If it's true . . . good grace . . . I'm exhausted! . . .

OLD ANGELA *(Trembling)*

Such an evening of unhappiness! . . . And the lantern ran out of oil . . .

MADAME *(Takes hold of the candle with determination.)*

Follow me! Don't waste time. He will look for another door, if he isn't inside already!

(The four women start for the corridor, and after they cross it, they go to the left and up a rotten staircase. Old Angela holds her rosary. Little Celestine cries and rubs her knee. At the top of the stairs, Madame leans against the banister and tries to listen.)

LITTLE CELESTINE *(Hesitating)*

Sounds like someone is coming up . . .

BIG MARTHA

It's the echo from the vault. It's nothing!

OLD ANGELA *(Trembling)*

Yes, someone is coming up. Even I who am a bit deaf can hear it, as certain as the words of the Bible! Holy Virgin! . . . Someone is coming up with a heavy footstep! . . . Watch out, Madame, we can't be safe except under the sky.

MADAME *(Lifting the candle)*

But we don't need to go downstairs again. Let's go to the balcony, since there is a set of stairs on each side . . .

(They cross yet another corridor, then they find themselves in front of a big door opening onto a wooden balcony. It is cold, the countryside is peaceful, but there is no moon.)

MADAME

By closing this door, we can't escape from him anymore, if he is inside! *(She tries to listen and looks behind her.)* So now then, my poor girls, courage! Try to listen, those of you whose ears are still good!

BIG MARTHA *(Whispering)*

I heard someone breathing!

OLD ANGELA

Me too!

LITTLE CELESTINE

Me too!

(Abruptly, the THREE SERVANTS run toward the balcony, BIG MARTHA and LITTLE CELESTINE descend the stairs like a whirlwind on one side, while OLD ANGELA, on the other side, descends as quickly as her old legs permit her. MADAME stops for a moment, overwhelmed, cold sweat running down her face. Finally, she cannot stand there anymore. She plants the candle on the threshold and hurries after Old Angela. And all these women, their arms up in the air, run to their chancy salvation, into a dark countryside, while, resembling a funeral light, the candle continues to burn on the gaping threshold of the abandoned house.)

Madame La Mort

A cerebral drama in three acts

First performance

Friday 20 March 1891

Théâtre d'Art

Characters

PAUL DARTIGNY

JACQUES DURAND

DOCTOR GODIN

JEAN

THE VEILED WOMAN

LUCIE

Notes on the characters

PAUL DARTIGNY is a young man between twenty-five and thirty, pale, tall, thin, with a delicate, weary face. His feverish eyes never look directly at the person to whom he speaks. Casual black suit, very close fitting, like a glove. At his neck, a woman's scarf. Paul is a cold man, easily exasperated.

JACQUES DURAND is a pleasant young man, the same age as Paul, a high school friend. Glowing pink face, alternately radiant or sullen, with no middle ground. He is dressed in style, with a hat, monocle, and cane. Affectation of great geniality.

LUCIE, the well-behaved "call girl" type. In company, respectable manners resembling those of a society woman. Elegant attire, cumbersome parasol. She speaks loudly, in a decided voice, and sometimes falls into a sort of forced sentimentality, which she fakes on purpose. A girl who likes well-bred gentlemen.

DOCTOR GODIN: Young, proper, well acquainted with death, which hardly bothers him. He speaks rapidly, with a clipped voice.

JEAN: Modern servant, *without a trace of the comic*. The dignified bearing of an office employee and not the foolish look of a flunkey who is there to make the audience laugh. He speaks carefully and properly.

THE VEILED WOMAN: Young, lithe woman, completely covered by a dust-gray veil over a long dress of the same gray.

Mournful voice, but clear and sharp. She never shows her feet, nor her hands, nor her face: she is an apparition. She walks, turns, moves, without a sound, like a shadow, but gracefully. She does not look like a ghost: she is not returning from the dead, she has never existed. She is an image, not a living being.

In the second act the symbolic character LIFE is played by LUCIE in a pink evening gown, with flowers, diamonds, and a fan. Her hair is loose.

The setting
The play takes place in Paris in the present.

Act One, Scene One

A very dark smoking room, draped in black. At left, in the back, a black sofa facing the audience. At right, a desk covered with papers, books, a cigar box, matches. At center, a small table covered with a black cloth, a small box on top of it. At the back, a double door. An enormous vase of mimosas on the mantel, at left, in front of a mirror. Armchairs and carpet, black with yellow brocade.

PAUL DARTIGNY *(Stands near the table, holding a little key in his hand. He puts the key into the lock of the box. He is alone. He speaks feverishly.)*

Will it be today? My nerves are terribly on edge from this cruel game . . . Oh, Madame, you always keep me waiting! This pointless flirtation makes you seem like a real woman . . .

Madame, please have pity on me . . . *(He plunges his hand into the box, turning his head away, as if afraid to see what he has touched. He pulls out a cigar which he examines carefully, then, deep in thought, he lets the lid fall back. An argument is heard behind the door at the back. The servant appears.)*

JEAN

Monsieur, I could not keep him from coming in . . .

PAUL DARTIGNY *(Impatiently)*

Who is it? I have already told you that I wish to receive no one, no one! . . .

(The servant leaves. JACQUES DURAND *appears at the doorway.)*

Act One. Scene Two

JACQUES DURAND

I see! You have shut yourself in now! You let me argue with your servant for an hour, and you are here all alone! *(He walks around the room.)* And all the little black ornaments! How cheerful! *(He stops in front of Paul who has hidden the cigar in his hand.)* But here I am, and I'm staying! *(He sits, puts his hat down, and taps his leg with an air of self-importance.)* Go ahead, make a face. I have made up my mind to take root in this chair until you take me by the shoulders and throw me out. I am very patient, you know . . .

PAUL DARTIGNY *(Smiling and sliding his cigar into his vest pocket, next to his chest)*
I know.

JACQUES DURAND

Look! What's the matter? Aren't you ashamed to hide from the light like an owl? Oh, my friend, it's a beautiful afternoon! Springtime! Sun! All you see out in the streets are flowers on lit-

tle carts and women in big hats . . . We are going out, the two
of us . . . You're not expecting anyone, are you? Besides, I have
something to say to you . . .

PAUL DARTIGNY

Go ahead.

JACQUES DURAND

Give me a cigar first.

PAUL DARTIGNY *(Goes to get a cigar box from his desk and offers it
to Jacques.)*

Choose one.

JACQUES DURAND *(Looking at them and making a face)*

Can't I taste the others then? . . . Yours . . . you know, those you
reserve for your personal use, you egomaniac . . . over there *(He
points to the box at the table.)* in that box which is always
locked, your servant says . . .

PAUL DARTIGNY *(He notices that he has left the key in the box,
and rushes over to it. He takes the key out and puts it in his pocket.)*

No! . . .

JACQUES DURAND

We have no manners anymore! *(He sits back down.)*

PAUL DARTIGNY *(Dreamily)*

Send you in my place and risk running into you again? That
would finish me.

JACQUES DURAND *(Astonished)*

You're going out? You have a date? *(Joyfully)* What will Lucie
say? . . . I'll go with you wherever you plan to go, I really will
. . . *(He gets up.)*

PAUL DARTIGNY *(Coldly)*

It's a long way.

JACQUES DURAND *(Grumbling)*

Another hoax, of course! *(He sits back down.)* You're not smoking anymore? *(He lights his cigar.)*

PAUL DARTIGNY

Yes, when I am alone . . . my special cigars . . . not all men relish the same smoke. *(He sits across from Jacques.)* You wanted to say something to me, Jacques?

JACQUES DURAND

Oh! . . . Nothing that will inconvenience you, I'm sure. I forced my way in here because I need five hundred francs: a trifle. I'll pay you back along with the rest, in a month or two.

PAUL DARTIGNY *(Gets up to go to his desk.)*

No trouble. *(He opens the drawer.)* Why didn't you say so, my friend? Giving occupies the mind. It is good to feel generous at certain times. I thank you for furnishing me with this final illusion . . . You want? . . . How much? . . . I have forgotten the amount.

JACQUES DURAND *(Offended)*

You are lucky, not to have to count your money! Seven hundred francs . . . But I'll pay you back: I give you my word. It's just . . . *(He counts on his fingers.)* the tailor, the club, Nini, and a big watch the size of a hazelnut, which I gave my dear little sister Angèle for her birthday . . . The little darling wanted it so much! . . . Don't sneer! I still have some family spirit, and I think everything can be taken care of: diamonds for Nini, so be it! . . . but a watch for that innocent young girl, my sister! *(He taps the ash off his cigar with a self-satisfied smile.)*

PAUL DARTIGNY *(Handing him the money)*

Here are your seven hundred francs, my friend. You have beautiful feelings which are a pleasure to witness, and for that I congratulate you.

JACQUES DURAND *(Putting the money in his wallet with satisfaction)*

Thank you. Don't laugh. You and your ironic remarks are unbearable.

PAUL DARTIGNY *(Gravely)*

I wouldn't know how to laugh. There is no reason!

JACQUES DURAND

I believe you, but you look like a man in a dream . . .

PAUL DARTIGNY

Forgive me. *(Smiling)* A dream is a stairway to the sky: I am very high, very far away . . . I no longer know where I am. *(He sits down again, his head turned away.)*

JACQUES DURAND

Spring fever. As for me, all my beautiful feelings, as you call them, are bursting up in my chest all at once, and I would like to find a chance to put them on display.

PAUL DARTIGNY *(Softly)*

The boutique on the thirteenth floor.

JACQUES DURAND *(Letting out great puffs of smoke)*

Just now I gave a coin to a beggar: ridiculous, eh? . . . I am going to pay off my debts . . . probably. *(He approaches Paul's chair.)* And I would like to cure you of your neuroses, take you out into the sunshine, to women, to the world . . . Help you, do you hear me! . . . You have had a dreadful winter: you must shake it off this summer, my dear Paul. *(He slaps Paul's shoulder.)*

PAUL DARTIGNY *(Lowering his head and looking at him, surprised)*

I don't like the sun.

JACQUES DURAND *(Crossing his arms.)*

You don't like the sun! *(Forcefully)* You are an absolute monster!

PAUL DARTIGNY

Ah! This theory is spread by devotees of the sun, since creatures of the moon are in the minority.

JACQUES DURAND *(Furious)*

You don't like the sun . . . Why, if you please?

PAUL DARTIGNY *(Calmly)*

The sun makes unpleasant creatures visible and I can't stand its arrogant attitude in the face of ghastly situations. It seems to me that the sun is like those drunks who come out of a wedding and force you to drink to the health of a bride . . . *(A pause)* whom you don't know.

JACQUES DURAND *(Laughing)*

All you have to do is pull the curtain, and it's gone! *(He shrugs his shoulders.)* Not to like the beauties of nature! I swear, he must be corrupted, completely corrupted.

PAUL DARTIGNY *(Containing himself)*

Oh, Jacques, Jacques. Let's not argue anymore! It is so trivial, these endless conversations about the tastes which you have and those which I have not. It would be better for each of us to stay home alone, I assure you.

JACQUES DURAND *(Sitting back down)*

You are most unpleasant! . . . After lending me money, it's not very polite, my dear friend.

PAUL DARTIGNY *(Looking at the ceiling)*

It's true . . . Pardon me, because I would like to believe that you are more and more inflated with beautiful sentiments. Nevertheless . . . I would prefer you . . . deflated.

JACQUES DURAND

Are you still on morphine these days?

PAUL DARTIGNY

No. I don't take drugs anymore. I am not such a coward as to keep using artificial means: I will go straight to the point.

JACQUES DURAND

And the point is?

PAUL DARTIGNY

You are very curious, my friend.

JACQUES DURAND *(Playing with his cane)*

Yesterday I ran into Doctor Godin, who expressly told me that you had taken a turn for the worse.

PAUL DARTIGNY *(With interest)*

Is that why you came here, Jacques?

JACQUES DURAND

For that and also for . . . the other thing . . . which I needed. I confess that your state of mind is more annoying than upsetting. Oh, if you were sick, with typhoid fever for instance, I could bring myself to sleep on this sofa and take care of you all night . . . But just between us, your case is more comical than dangerous: it's an imaginary illness.

PAUL DARTIGNY

Why would typhoid fever be more dangerous than an illness of my imagination, my dear friend?

JACQUES DURAND

You would be in danger of dying, for heaven's sake!

PAUL DARTIGNY *(With a mocking laugh)*

You all fear death almost as if you worship it.

JACQUES DURAND

But my dear, dear friend, personally, that's all I fear! *(He stands up.)* What else should we all fear if not that?

PAUL DARTIGNY *(In a calm voice)*

> Death is a woman. I see no reason not to enjoy her company.
> It's that simple.

JACQUES DURAND

> You are talking gibberish. *(Getting excited)* Either you have
> some love story on your brain, or you're just arrogant, and a
> good catastrophe, a real illness will cure you better than all our
> sermons would. Listen, my dear Paul, at bottom you are an
> egotist: you give because you don't need anything, you don't
> like women anymore because you had a lot of women, you
> don't like society anymore because you were part of it whenever
> you wanted . . . Yes, an egotist! And the proof, your cigars
> locked up for the past two weeks. Even your servant is dis-
> gusted by that behavior: you act as if you don't trust him . . .
> You're putting up a big smokescreen. Bored with life? Come on!
> At your age? . . . I am an old friend: I am going to drag the
> whole truth out of you. *(A pause)* The truth is your pride is
> hurt. You have tried every social circle, one after another, and
> they have all turned you down. *(He counts on his fingers.)* You
> frequented artists: you failed. You frequented salons: you don't
> even know English. You frequented women: they don't like you
> . . . Aside from Lucie, you haven't got a hope. My friend, your
> misfortune is that you squandered your wealth to gain knowl-
> edge instead of living an honest life. Your famous pessimism
> only serves to throw powder in our eyes and it's nothing but a
> bad education: not to live like the rest of the world is sheer
> impoliteness, everyone tells you so . . . You, the *blasés*, the
> hypochondriacs, you simply have bad manners . . . Personally,
> when I eat beef, I resent watching my neighbor ask for veal.
> After all, what are you complaining about? You're rich, an
> orphan, free, without a wife . . . and without a mother-in-law.

PAUL DARTIGNY *(Looking at the ceiling, no longer listening)*

What's the matter with him? What mother-in-law? His words ring in my ears like a death knell . . . But unfortunately, now it strikes me that even a death knell can be ridiculous.

JACQUES DURAND *(Grasping his arm)*

I insist that you be happy to be alive, do you hear me! . . . Godin says that you must have stolen poison from him and this will lead to trouble. The doctor really said so, believe me. You're not going to play a bad trick like suicide, are you? And Lucie, that pretty girl, that treasure of grace and beauty, who, I am sure, doesn't cost you as much as a society woman, how do you know what she does when you are away from her, when you shut yourself up for a whole week with your daydreams? . . . Oh, those horrible daydreams, if I could catch them! . . . *(Menacing gesture)*

PAUL DARTIGNY *(Coldly)*

What she does? . . . I have no idea. Try to restrain yourself from telling me, please . . . Oh, the sound of your voice gets on my nerves, like a needle, Jacques. My syringe of Pravaz is preferable.

JACQUES DURAND *(Solemnly)*

There is one thing, Paul.

PAUL DARTIGNY

What, my friend?

JACQUES DURAND *(Pointing his finger sententiously)*

In depravity, there is Pravaz! *(Happily)* That joke is good enough for the Club.

PAUL DARTIGNY *(He rubs his forehead and stands)*

And in the bourgeois soul, there always sleeps . . . an old gossip columnist.

JACQUES DURAND *(Exasperated)*

Come on! . . . Bourgeois, we are all bourgeois: you, me, Lucie, Godin, and the grocer across the street!

PAUL DARTIGNY

I am afraid you will even have children.

JACQUES DURAND

. . . Who, let's hope, won't be like you—deranged!

PAUL DARTIGNY *(Philosophically)*

Especially if they are Lucie's.

JACQUES DURAND

No, I assure you, Lucie is very attached to you. She is a nice girl, quite without malice.

PAUL DARTIGNY

Like you: you were made for each other! *(Dry laugh)*

JACQUES DURAND *(Uneasily)*

You're not suspicious of me, I hope . . . Look, we're alone: how much do you pay her?

PAUL DARTIGNY *(Gesture of suppressed rage)*

Oh! I don't know! I pay her?

JACQUES DURAND

She is elegant! . . . Oh! Style . . . purity of lines . . .

PAUL DARTIGNY

She is like the lily from the Bible . . . She spins sometimes and saves up a lot . . . a very common flower, all in all.

JACQUES DURAND

So, what do you expect? . . . You would deserve it if I flirted with her right in front of you, my friend, in revenge for your stupid contempt. Luckily, I still have respect for my friendships.

PAUL DARTIGNY *(In a heavy voice)*

All I ask of you is not to flirt . . . or make love to her in front of my eyes . . . while I watch.

JACQUES DURAND *(In an outburst)*

You are becoming coarse . . . Just now you were blasphemous!

PAUL DARTIGNY *(Surprised)*

Blasphemous?

JACQUES DURAND *(Serious)*

You spoke about the bourgeois a moment ago . . . Well, the bourgeois, and I am one of them, we have one virtue: we believe in God . . . from time to time.

PAUL DARTIGNY

Which separates you from the beasts, I know! My compliments!

JACQUES DURAND *(Going back and forth, very excited)*

Bourgeois! It's a mouthful, that word! . . . What do you mean by this sort of insult anyway?

PAUL DARTIGNY

You said it yourself: you, me, Lucie, Godin, the grocer across the street . . . Or even *(Stressing his words)* a man whose feet are on the ground, a man who seems better balanced than the others . . . But when he stumbles he crushes everything, and when he falls he never gets back up. Are you happy?

JACQUES DURAND *(Sadly)*

My name is Jacques Durand: it's bourgeois, I feel it, all right! A label like that classifies you forever. One of my aunts wanted to baptize me Gaëtano! I'm sorry no one listened: Gaëtano is even better than Carolus . . .

PAUL DARTIGNY *(Smiling)*

You miss Gaëtano.

JACQUES DURAND

Don't laugh, Paul! Your mother must have had aspirations like that, too. All our mothers were romantics.

PAUL DARTIGNY *(Gloomy)*

My mother . . . *(Musing)* She was a gentle soul who suffered everything . . . *(A pause)* and understood nothing! . . . As a child when I leaned my head against her heart, I felt the sound of her sighs the way one can hear, behind a curtain of crumpled silk, a wind that moans, blindly, in the night . . .

JACQUES DURAND *(Laughing)*

The poor soul evidently liked silk dresses, since her blouse rustled in such a pleasant manner . . . And your father? *(He relights his cigar.)* He was a bon vivant, it seems to me?

PAUL DARTIGNY *(Coldly)*

A very distinguished gentleman: he used to seduce our maids.

JACQUES DURAND

Shut up, my dear friend. All our fathers did the same thing, and we owe them our respect!

(JEAN comes in.)

Act One, Scene Three

JEAN

Sir, Doctor Godin is here. He is in a hurry.

PAUL DARTIGNY *(Shrugging his shoulders)*

Another one! . . . Let him in, if he is in a hurry . . . Perhaps I am at the point of death.

(DOCTOR GODIN comes in from the door at the back at a brisk pace. He gives a rapid handshake to Jacques Durand and speaks in his ear.)

JACQUES DURAND *(Out loud)*

So, you still hold to your opinion? . . . I examined him from every angle . . . I think he's fooling us. He doesn't have any poison, I assure you, my dear doctor.

DOCTOR GODIN *(Quite calm, he puts his hat on the table and stands facing Paul.)*

My dear friend, no arguments, since I have a patient waiting. From shelf number 5 of my consulting room, someone has taken a vial with the number 9,698 and a green stopper, containing a brown liquid. Now, firstly, you are obsessed with suicide. Secondly, I have no confidence in the integrity of madmen of your type, at least as far as dangerous drugs are concerned. Thirdly, you will return my vial, because nerium oleander is a costly poison. Conclusion: if I had an hour to waste today, I would insult you, and end by exchanging the customary pair of seconds . . . Do not lie, my friend, I am certain of it: you have a wrinkle in the middle of your forehead . . .

JACQUES DURAND *(Carried away)*

The medical examination didn't take long at all! Godin, you are priceless.

PAUL DARTIGNY

I wouldn't lie about anything so petty . . . Yes, it's the truth, I did steal the poison from you. *(He goes to his desk.)* How much do I owe you?

DOCTOR GODIN *(Angry)*

Damn it! What did you do with it?

JACQUES DURAND *(Jumping back)*

Oh! This is not possible! . . . What did you do with it, you idiot?

(A moment of silence)

PAUL DARTIGNY *(In a very gentle voice)*

So . . . you absolutely refuse to leave me alone, both of you?

DOCTOR GODIN *(Tapping his hat)*

My dear friend, are you making fun of me? I am in a hurry, and I cannot sell you the poison because of the police . . . They are amazing, these neurotics! You would put me in a fine pickle . . . if you were dead! . . . Now, hurry up and return it to me . . . I give you ten minutes.

PAUL DARTIGNY *(With dignity)*

One minute will suffice, my dear Godin. *(He points to the box on the table.)* I threw one poisoned cigar in there along with thirty harmless Havanas. Look for it. As for me, I have been expecting it for two weeks now. I wanted to achieve the supreme climax of a rendezvous with Death . . . But Lady Death, my Lady, has not appeared yet . . . To make herself desirable is part of her role as a woman, after all.

(GODIN seizes the box and puts it under his arm, while JACQUES lets out a cry and immediately throws down his cigar.)

DOCTOR GODIN

Splendid! . . . Only demented poets commit suicide with poisoned cigars! . . . How the fin-de-siècle mocks us with this business! . . . In the morning, Monsieur Lover-of-Death, you would have paid the price! . . . Between us, I advise you to hang yourself, it is more amusing, because nerium oleander makes one go a little insane and it has a rather bitter taste . . . My dear Dartigny, I have the honor of wishing you good day. Monsieur Durand . . . *(He shakes Durand's hand.)*

JACQUES DURAND *(Seizing his cane)*

I'm going with you, doctor!

PAUL DARTIGNY *(With an ironic wave of farewell)*

Bon voyage! *(He moves away from them, then pulls the cigar from his vest pocket and lights it.)* I, too, want to depart. With this cigar, they leave me a last chance for escape . . . and the opportunity to prove my egotism . . . if I am an egotist. *(He smokes.)*

(GODIN *and* JACQUES, *already in the doorway, move back to allow* LUCIE *to pass through. The doctor steps aside; Jacques bows ceremoniously.)*

JACQUES DURAND

It is a pleasure to see you, Mademoiselle. You look lovely . . .

DOCTOR GODIN

Let's hurry, please. Good day, Madame.

(The two men exit. Then JACQUES DURAND *comes back in and, from the threshold, calls out to Paul, who is still standing with his back turned.)*

JACQUES DURAND

I am going with the doctor and bringing back a carriage. We'll drive to the park together: this will take our minds off the problem. Until later, Mademoiselle.

Act One, Scene Four

LUCIE   *(Lifting her veil)*

What problem? *(The door closes again.)*

PAUL DARTIGNY   *(Smoking dreamily)*

Will she come?

LUCIE   *(Astonished)*

You were waiting for me, my little Paul? *(She puts her arms around his neck.)* Were you really waiting for me? . . . *(Exaggerated caresses.)* Answer me, come on.

PAUL DARTIGNY

Perhaps . . . I am waiting for a veiled woman. Why do you take off your veil?

LUCIE *(Irritated)*

Don't tease. You never wait for me!

PAUL DARTIGNY *(Smiling)*

Lord, no more than the spring, and you always return.

LUCIE *(Offering him her lips)*

You are really annoying with your jokes . . . Come on, try to act nice.

PAUL DARTIGNY

This smoke doesn't bother you?

LUCIE *(Shrugging her shoulders)*

As if I'm not used to it, with all of you! *(She kisses him.)*

PAUL DARTIGNY *(Letting out a cry and jumping back. Expression of joy mixed with terror.)*

Oh! Don't kiss me anymore . . . My lips are bitter . . . At last! You are here, Madame! . . . *(He draws further back.)* Oh, Lucie, didn't you see a gray shawl floating . . . in this smoke . . . around us? The unknowable woman is passing by! . . . I saw her as clearly as I see you . . . *(He hides his face in his hands.)* Oh, it's terrifying and divine! . . . Lucie! I swear to you that I saw her as I see you . . . there, behind you . . . just the way I have dreamed her . . .

LUCIE *(Losing her temper)*

You have taken drugs, haven't you? You took morphine, and you will fall asleep or say crazy things to me . . . *(She throws herself into an armchair.)* Life with you is so delightful!

PAUL DARTIGNY *(Goes toward her with a bewildered look.)*

Can you smell the fragrance of withered roses? *(Animated)* Where are the roses? Where are the roses? . . . In your corsage or in my heart? *(He looks carefully at Lucie.)*

LUCIE *(Tapping her foot and twisting the handle of her parasol)*

Me? . . . I have perfume on my handkerchief, that's all.

PAUL DARTIGNY *(Straightens up and begins smoking again.)*

No doubt: a perfumed handkerchief is a very vulgar luxury . . . *(He struggles against a slight dizziness.)* Forgive me, Lucie, I am a little ill and I am treating you badly. My nerves are on edge. First, the sound of Jacques's voice . . . Then yours . . . which grates on me like your diamonds shining in bathroom mirrors . . . *(He staggers and crosses his hands over his chest.)* You have clawed at my soul with all your nails . . . *(He falls into an armchair.)* Do you think about death sometimes, Lucie?

LUCIE *(In a hissing voice)*

Always joking! . . . Oh, do I ever want to walk out on you!

PAUL DARTIGNY *(Standing back up, distraught)*

Go get me a glass of water, Lucie. There is a horrible bitterness in my mouth . . .

LUCIE

I am not your maid! . . . *(She stands and goes to fix her hair in front of the mirror.)*

PAUL DARTIGNY *(Kneeling on a chair near her)*

You are cruel, my dear . . . *(Very softly)* You are charming . . . fresh and painted like Life . . . I took care of you in my will, you know . . . *(LUCIE turns and smiles.)* You deign to smile, your eyes light up . . . We are all mortal, my darling . . . Beautiful eyes! . . . Yes, your eyes are a crystal over an abyss, and I who have leaned over them, I have glimpsed truth . . . I thought I loved you more than Death, and you brought me to nothingness and repose . . . You threw me into her arms. I bless you. *(He kisses her hands.)*

LUCIE *(Laughing)*

What great style you have, telling yourself stories! . . . A first class burial, huh!

PAUL DARTIGNY *(Smoking and speaking slowly)*

I am afraid, Lucie . . . I am very ill and I wouldn't want to seem insistent, but . . . you have come at the same time as She. It is not my fault . . . Do you need me, Lucie?

LUCIE *(Tidying her clothes and speaking very quickly)*

Darling, I want to move to Monceau Park. The total will be three thousand francs.

PAUL DARTIGNY *(Delirious)*

I will fill my tomb with gold and precious stones . . . Come with me, if you dare.

LUCIE *(Scornfully)*

Where do you want to make me go? . . . The country, like last fall? . . . Not before the Grand Prix, you understand! . . . I know them, your tombs full of gold and precious stones . . . An empty house, huge beds that make you cold down to your bones, and it rains all day long . . . Thanks. No one's going to catch me at that game again!

PAUL DARTIGNY *(Sinking down on his knees)*

Oh! I saw red flames . . . The terror! . . . *(He hides his face in Lucie's dress for a moment.)* I feel like a little sick child, and every woman should be a mother to a man in pain . . . Lucie, I saw sparks burning on this carpet! Have pity . . . *(He lies at her feet.)* I would love you so much if you only kept quiet!

LUCIE *(Giggling)*

But you're drunk! . . . That stuff must be good! . . . What did you have to drink? . . . You are drunk, Paul!

PAUL DARTIGNY *(Gets back up, exasperated.)*

> What did I have to drink? . . . You idiot, I have drained the
> whole chalice! . . . I am satiated with life! . . . Get out of here!
> . . . Let me sleep . . .

LUCIE *(She shakes her head as she looks at him.)*

> Being alone with him, it's not very safe. He's going crazy . . .
> Look, Paul, let's talk more seriously . . . Those three thousand
> francs, I need them . . . It's not funny, I mean it . . . Paul! . . .
> *(Shouting)* Paul! . . .

PAUL DARTIGNY *(Moves across the room, holding onto the furniture. When he gets to the sofa at the back, he speaks wildly.)*

> Who is calling me? . . . Is it my beloved? . . . *(He sinks down on
> the sofa.)*

LUCIE

> Oh! I've had enough of your stories about strange women!

(Noise behind the door. The servant comes in.)

Act One, Scene Five

JEAN

> It's Monsieur Jacques Durand again.

(He leaves.)

(JACQUES DURAND comes in.)

JACQUES DURAND *(Bows.)*

> I am not disturbing you?

LUCIE *(Enraged)*

> Disturbing us! . . . Come on, look at him: he is falling asleep in
> front of me. He is asleep on his feet! . . . Oh! He ought to be
> slapped! . . .

JACQUES DURAND *(Smiling)*

> Morphine, his consolation! . . . .You can't always get what you want . . . Godin agrees with you, Mademoiselle, we must give him a talking to . . . and it's more urgent than you can imagine . . . *(Irritated)* And I was just bringing a carriage! . . .

LUCIE *(Furious, she goes to the sofa where Dartigny lies.)*

> One . . . Two . . . You are not coming? . . . You don't want to come? . . . *(Pause)* Fine, I am going to the park with him! . . . Are you coming? . . . *(She takes Jacques's arm.)* Good night!

JACQUES DURAND *(Bowing)*

> We won't be back until dinner.

(They exit.)

PAUL DARTIGNY *(Trying to sit up)*

> Don't make a sound . . . Oh, don't make a sound . . . I can smell the fragrance of withered roses.

Act Two, Scene One

A garden on a spring day in soft, hazy light. Banks of light-colored shrubs and rose bushes. Dominating the stage in the back, a cypress shrouded in mist. At center, a stone bench that looks like a tomb.

PAUL DARTIGNY *(Stretched out on the ground in a rigid pose, his head leaning against the stone bench. He is very pale and seems to be asleep. Then he wakes and murmurs in a faint voice.)*

> . . . Withered roses . . . *(He sits up.)* What country is this? . . . Why am I in this strange garden? . . . *(He stands up, his hand on his forehead.)* My head is light and cold like a snowflake, and yet my body feels very heavy . . . *(He takes several wavering steps, looks around, then smiles.)* It is absurd . . . and charming . . .

LUCIE'S VOICE *(Far away)*

> Paul! . . . Paul! . . .

PAUL DARTIGNY *(Listening)*

> That tearful voice makes my blood run cold . . . Yes, I inhabit
> the country of the ultimate fantasy . . . Here, every dark illu-
> sion will attack me . . . Am I only sleeping, or am I already
> dead? . . . The scent of these flowers has a disturbing subtlety:
> they try to dissuade me, they offer me their pious lies, and yet
> . . . I sense in them . . . a terrifying smell of earth . . .

LUCIE'S VOICE *(Nearer)*

> Paul! . . . Paul! . . .

PAUL DARTIGNY

> Lord! She again! Always she! . . . *(He clasps his hands above his
> head.)* Ah, Madame, you my great beloved, you the comforter,
> you the Absolute, come to my aid! . . . A terrible thing is about
> to happen, I foresee it: I must witness the hour of my death . . .
> *(Recoiling)* If I could see your face! . . . If I could only touch you!
> . . . *(Moment of silence.)* No more . . . She no longer calls my
> name . . . I am dead already . . . Forgotten . . . *(He falls back on
> the stone bench and looks at the garden.)* Oh, what a ravishing
> country! . . . The air here is as sweet as honey . . . I want to stay
> here, to get drunk from the sweetness all around . . . then sleep,
> I am very tired . . . I have walked for thirty years! . . .

LUCIE'S VOICE *(Very close)*

> Paul! . . . *(LUCIE comes out from the grove. She wears a pink
> evening gown, loosely draped, and a diamond necklace. Her hair is
> loose and she holds a fan.)* Paul! . . .

(PAUL DARTIGNY shudders and stands up, his eyes blank.)

Act Two, Scene Two

LUCIE *(Runs to Paul and throws herself at his feet.)*

> You want to leave me, but you said I was your life!

PAUL DARTIGNY *(With difficulty, turning his head away)*

It is true, I did say you were my life . . . I cursed you too, do
you remember that? In those days, you were my lover. But now
step back and let the supreme ecstasy appear: you are nothing
to me anymore . . . *She* is here, I know it, near us . . . Don't
argue with her over my body, since you did not know how to
hold on to my soul . . . *(He tries to push her away.)* What
demon wants to show me life in the face of a lover . . . *(Angrily)*
who abandons me?

LUCIE *(Still on her knees, hanging on to Paul's hands)*

No. You belong to me! *(Fiercely)* I'll cling to your body the way
ivy still clings to a tree cut at the root . . . I won't let you fall
into the abyss . . . I feasted for so long on your flesh and blood
that now I am the stronger. I love you! . . .

PAUL DARTIGNY *(Sadly)*

Oh, vain words! . . . This is a part you must have played for so
many other men! . . . Enough, get out of here! *(Harshly)* You
make me sick . . .

LUCIE

What can I do to prove my love to you?

PAUL DARTIGNY

Stop it! . . . *(He turns away toward the back of the stage, then
recoils with a hollow cry: he has just seen, standing against the
cypress, a gray form shrouded in mist.)*

Act Two. Scene Three

LUCIE *(Still on her knees, reaching out to him)*

Come back, Paul! . . . I am mistress, I am wife, I am mother
. . . You have no right to run from me . . . I order you to stay.
(Noticing the gray silhouette, she stands up and rushes to him.)
Oh! That hideous woman! . . . My rival, Paul! . . .

PAUL DARTIGNY *(Curtly)*

Yes!

LUCIE *(Enraged)*

He is insane! *(She holds him in her arms.)*

PAUL DARTIGNY *(Continuing to look at the Veiled Woman, who comes forward slowly, slowly, but not as if walking: she is gliding. He pleads.)*

Save me, Madame, if you are She whom I await! . . . Save me, I implore you! . . .

THE VEILED WOMAN *(Closer and closer, moving out of the mist)*

Soon!

LUCIE *(Beside herself)*

Miserable phantom who subverts the healthiest minds and turns the most noble hearts to ice, where have you come from? . . . Oh! I will protect him from your black magic! . . . I have the power of desire, and the flesh I have kissed so often will surely rebel at your touch . . .

THE VEILED WOMAN *(Gliding a step forward, while Paul shrinks back, still in Lucie's grip)*

The flesh you have kissed for so long will rot more quickly.

PAUL DARTIGNY *(Trying to break free)*

I am in agony . . . Madame, have pity on my suffering . . . It is only a courtesan drunk on her own words . . .

LUCIE *(Tightening her grip)*

Don't worry, I won't let you go now! I hold you, we are one . . . *(She turns to the Veiled Woman.)* Between your ugliness and my beauty, what do you think he will choose, you rambling old princess?

THE VEILED WOMAN *(Gliding a step forward)*

It is not for him to choose: you are his body, but I am his soul.

LUCIE *(Speaking passionately to Paul)*

You thought I was pretty once. . . *(She shows herself off.)* Look at me, I have all my diamonds . . .

THE VEILED WOMAN *(Gliding a step forward)*

Indeed all the tears he shed since he was born sparkle at your throat.

LUCIE *(Pleading)*

My dress is pink: it was spun from the dawn . . .

THE VEILED WOMAN

You made your dress by tearing off his skin . . .

LUCIE *(Fanning herself.)*

I fan myself with April breezes . . .

THE VEILED WOMAN *(Still advancing toward Paul)*

Your fan is fever's wing.

LUCIE *(Leaning on Dartigny, who sobs.)*

I break open the shells of birds' eggs with my delicate nails.

THE VEILED WOMAN

She bloodies forests when she is in heat.

LUCIE *(More insistant)*

Remember my expert ways of pleasure. One night, the stars left the sky because they didn't dare look at us anymore.

THE VEILED WOMAN *(Still advancing)*

And, defeated by fatigue, he fell into a sleep as heavy . . . as my arm. *(She lifts her right arm.)*

LUCIE

You make me laugh.

THE VEILED WOMAN *(Now quite close to Paul)*

You may well laugh now . . .

LUCIE *(Covering Paul with kisses)*

You loved me so much!

THE VEILED WOMAN *(Coming between Paul and Lucie)*

You deceived him so much!

PAUL DARTIGNY *(Writhing in pain)*

Have pity, Madame, end my suffering! . . . *(He sobs.)* Her hair was so long! . . . *(He looks at Lucie.)*

THE VEILED WOMAN *(Wraps Paul in her veil.)*

My veil is even longer.

LUCIE *(Shrinks back, struck with fear.)*

Paul, I would have given you beautiful children.

THE VEILED WOMAN *(With a scornful gesture, leaning on the young man's shoulder)*

Wretched woman! You kill love with this idea of procreation, because love is the only god who cannot multiply without vanishing. Ridiculous whore, you trade your kisses for the base coin of pain! You are an animal who drowns pleasure in dung. And your children are pledged to me from their cradle. Unnatural mother, without logic and without purpose, living in daylight and denying the night. Go! For him you were a useless servant whom he paid too dearly!

LUCIE *(Shrinks back to the stone bench and calls in despair.)*

Paul! . . . Paul! . . . *(With a weaker voice)* Paul! . . . Paul! . . . *(Faintly)* Paul! . . . *(She disappears behind the roses.)* Paul! . . .

Act Two, Scene Four

PAUL DARTIGNY *(One knee on the ground, in front of the Veiled Woman)*

Thank you, oh my sovereign and only love! Allow me to bow before you. I was nothing but dust. I return to dust. *(He kisses*

the hem of her veil.) You are finally here, mysterious woman. I
waited for you at every nightfall . . . I have dreamed of your
beauty: will I never see you?

THE VEILED WOMAN *(Softly)*

No!

PAUL DARTIGNY *(Timidly and with love)*

The breeze here caresses . . . It sways the flowers, Madame, and
your veil is very light . . .

THE VEILED WOMAN

I do not stop the breeze: it passes through me.

PAUL DARTIGNY *(Horrified)*

Do not say that, my queen, you will freeze my blood.

THE VEILED WOMAN

It is already frozen.

PAUL DARTIGNY *(Stands, and, led by her, reaches the bench, where
he sits. She remains standing at his side. He takes her hands.)*

My love! . . . Forgive me, my mouth is still bitter with Life's
kisses . . . I am impure. You will purify me.

THE VEILED WOMAN

By burning your bones.

PAUL DARTIGNY

What will become of my soul, this soul which belongs to you?
. . . Is there a God?

THE VEILED WOMAN *(Pointing towards the sky)*

Watch the turtle doves glide: what do they need except sweet
air and sunny weather?

PAUL DARTIGNY *(Tenderly)*

You are a woman, because you speak in riddles, my cruel
fiancée! . . . But is there eternal love?

THE VEILED WOMAN *(Pointing to a rose bush)*

See how these roses shed their petals: they take longer to dry
. . . than a woman's tears.

PAUL DARTIGNY *(Stands.)*

Where you live, is it at least permitted to know pride?

THE VEILED WOMAN

There is no greater pride than silence.

PAUL DARTIGNY

Must I be quiet?

THE VEILED WOMAN

You only imagine you speak.

PAUL DARTIGNY *(With despair)*

Oh, horrible dream! . . . To hear her, to touch her, and not to
know if it is She! . . . *(A moment of silence)* Into what exquisite
turmoil this creature of darkness throws me! . . . Will I die or
live? Will I find emptiness beneath this veil, or royal beauty?
. . . *(He approaches her.)* Tell me, might I sometimes, sleepless in
our shadowy bed, press your form against my chest, like the
body of a woman . . . who would resist? . . .

THE VEILED WOMAN

I represent the end of these vanities. You will sleep.

PAUL DARTIGNY

I will sleep deeply! *(Joyfully)* For how many centuries?

THE VEILED WOMAN

Do you know the number of centuries since you met me?. . .
Action has ended and time is no more.

PAUL DARTIGNY

At last, can you tell me who you are, you, Death?

THE VEILED WOMAN *(In a very hollow voice)*

I do not know.

PAUL DARTIGNY *(Transported)*

I adore you, and you are ravishing, my beloved! . . . *(He puts his head on the Veiled Woman's chest and falls back on the bench, half-asleep.)*

THE VEILED WOMAN *(Sweetly)*

Come, the hour is here, the nuptial bed is ready. Sleep, my unhappy lover. *(She wraps him in her arms and in her veil.)*

PAUL DARTIGNY *(Faintly)*

Let us sleep . . . together, is it not . . . together . . .

THE VEILED WOMAN *(Softly, spreading out once and for all the folds of her veil)*

Forever.

Act Three, Scene One

Same scene as Act One. Paul Dartigny, dead, lying on the sofa at the back. Half-darkness at the rise of the curtain.

JEAN *(Enters through the door at the back.)*

Monsieur! . . . Monsieur! . . . *(He goes up to the sofa.)* Very good, here he is, fast asleep! . . . And the other two are over there in the living room, in the midst of . . . kissing each other probably . . . What a dog's life! . . . With this maniac here, you never know which end is up . . . *(Louder)* Monsieur! . . . *(He leans over the sofa.)* He is sleeping with his eyes open now . . . *(Uneasy)* Drugs these days will do this to you . . . But what's the difference, his eyes look funny anyway! . . . Monsieur! . . . *(He lifts Paul's arm, which falls back down limp.)* What! . . . *(He is confused.)*

JACQUES DURAND *(Behind the door at the back, knocking with his cane)*

We are here, my friend, and Mademoiselle Lucie *(Burst of suppressed laughter)* is very hungry, I assure you . . . *(Raising his voice)* If you make us wait, you are just a coward! . . . *(More laughter)*

JEAN *(Raising his arms)*

Lord! It's too much! *(Shocked)* I think he must be . . . dead! . . . I have no job, and the police will interrogate me! . . .

Act Three. Scene Two

JACQUES DURAND *(Enters with Lucie, who carries a bunch of flowers.)*

Well? . . . Are we still sleeping off the morphine? . . . *(The servant stops him and puts a finger over his mouth, looking toward Lucie.)* What? . . . What's the matter? . . . Is he still asleep?

JEAN *(Nodding his head)*

I think so, Monsieur. *(He goes towards the door.)* I am going now . . . If you need my services . . . *(He leaves.)*

JACQUES DURAND *(Surprised)*

That Jean is strange! . . .

LUCIE *(Putting the flowers in a vase)*

Now you see, my dear Durand, it's unbearable! Even his servant is crazy!

JACQUES DURAND *(Biting the handle of his cane)*

My poor dear! Well, we won't get to eat dinner together?

LUCIE

No. I don't want to make a scene. *(She takes off her hat.)* Must be sensible . . . *(She goes up to the sofa and leans over the corpse.)* Come on, Paul, you are making fun of us, aren't you? . . . I am hungry, it's dinner time!

JACQUES DURAND *(Grumbling)*

It must be even more pleasant when they are alone! . . .*(He lowers his voice.)* Lucie! . . . Lucie! . . . Remember our walk in the park, when . . . you wanted . . . to acquire . . . a new . . . *(He hesitates.)* friend.

LUCIE *(Smiles at Jacques.)*

Jean! . . . Bring us a lamp.

JEAN *(Coming in almost immediately, with a large candelabrum filled with lighted candles)*

Here, Madame. *(He puts the candelabrum on the table.)*

LUCIE *(Irritated)*

I asked for a lamp, not this altar piece!

(JEAN leaves the room very quickly, while watching Lucie return to the sofa. She looks at Paul Dartigny, then lets out a horrible scream, and runs to the other end of the room.)

JACQUES DURAND *(Frightened)*

What's the matter, Lucie? . . . Paul, what have you done to her? . . . *(In turn, he goes and leans over the sofa.)* Oh! Lord, these staring eyes . . . this pallor . . . But . . . *(He recoils.)* But he is dead! . . . *(A moment of silence. Lucie falls on her knees and buries her face in her dress.)* Help! . . . Oh! It's not possible! . . . *(He runs to the door.)* Jean! . . . A doctor! . . . Jean . . . *(The servant comes in right away.)*

JEAN *(In a respectful tone of voice)*

Is something wrong, Monsieur Durand?

JACQUES DURAND *(Showing him the corpse)*

He is dead! . . . He was killed!

LUCIE *(She rolls on the carpet, in hysterics.)*

Help! . . . Help! . . .

JEAN *(Running to the sofa)*

It's the drugs! . . . He must have taken too much . . . Poor Monsieur! I really think you are right. He doesn't look well.

JACQUES DURAND *(Dazed, he walks around the room while Lucie drags herself along holding onto the furniture.)*

It's horrible . . . horrible! . . . My poor friend! Like that, all alone, and we thought we had saved him today! . . . Jean, keep it quiet: we don't want the neighbors on our hands . . . Lord! Lucie, calm down. *(He helps her up and places her in an armchair.)* Quiet! . . . Don't scream, I beg you . . . Jean, go get Doctor Godin. He will know what to do! . . . Paul must have committed suicide . . . In any case, I don't know any more than anybody else! . . . Try and do something, Jean . . . Get vinegar . . . Rub his hands . . . *(Jean goes out.)* So that our conscience is clear at least! . . . Come on, Lucie, come on now! . . . *(A moment of silence. Only Lucie's sobs can be heard.)* You loved him that much! . . .

(JEAN comes back bringing a decanter and a cloth. He goes over to the corpse.)

LUCIE *(Wringing her hands)*

Lord! I am so afraid! . . . *(She tries to breathe.)* Monsieur Durand, don't leave! . . . Oh, those eyes, that mouth . . . Poor Paul! . . . That it should end like this! I knew it would! . . . *(She cries.)* I am so unfortunate . . .

JACQUES DURAND

Yes, we are truly to be pitied.

JEAN *(Composes himself and speaks in a restrained voice.)*

Monsieur Jacques, there is nothing to be done: he is cold . . . But we could search the drawers: a suicide always leaves some sort of explanation.

JACQUES DURAND *(No longer daring to look in the direction of the sofa)*

My knees are shaking, Jean. Search if you dare. As for me, I can do no more . . . *(He leans against Lucie's armchair.)* A dead man

in a room, it's like a punch in the stomach . . . *(He shivers.)* No,
I can do no more . . . I was his best friend . . .

LUCIE *(In a panic, clutching Jacques's jacket)*

You must not leave me! I would be terrified . . . Don't you
think they could accuse us of killing him?

JACQUES DURAND *(Trying to breathe)*

You are losing your mind! . . . Why would we have killed him?
(Tenderly) We all loved him, you, me, his servant.

JEAN *(Covering the dead man's face with the cloth)*

I should go get Doctor Godin then?

JACQUES DURAND

Go quickly, my friend. Bring him right away: we cannot stay
here, Madame and I . . . We may be accountable . . . A suicide
is a serious matter, very serious . . . *(A pause)* Because usually
the police get involved.

(JEAN leaves.)

LUCIE *(Wiping her eyes)*

What will become of me?

JACQUES DURAND

Poor little girl! . . . *(He clasps her hands.)* Be brave. You won't be
without friends . . . *(He lowers his voice.)* Did Dartigny ever
used to talk about a . . . will, in the middle of his fits of melan-
choly?

LUCIE *(With her hand on her forehead)*

Yes, I think he made one . . . Wait a moment, he was talking to
me about it this afternoon . . . *(She gets up.)* There, in the desk
. . . the right hand drawer. *(She turns towards the sofa.)* His face
is covered. I like it better that way. *(She tries to walk a few steps.)*
Oh! I was so terrified! . . . I thought he was laughing in my face

. . . *(Frightened)* and he was dead! . . . *(She leans on Jacques's shoulder and walks to the desk.)*

JACQUES DURAND

Be careful . . . You never know what they can accuse us of . . . This is a terrible situation.

LUCIE *(Rummaging through the drawer)*

Look, here is a letter for me . . . Ah, never mind, I am opening it . . . It's not the will, but maybe it talks about it. Anyway, it is addressed to me. *(She reads.)* "My dear child, I cost you many smiles, and in leaving you the rest of my fortune, I remain your debtor. I hope my suicide will cause you no pain. I beg you to write nothing on my tombstone: if this does not seem too preposterous, my dear child, in six months, you will share my opinion. Your humble servant, Paul Dartigny. Postscript: My will is at Monsieur Varin's, notary, 23, Bethune Street." *(She breaks into sobs.)* The poor man! . . . He was crazy!

JACQUES DURAND *(Pensive)*

Yes, crazy indeed . . . When life is so beautiful!

LUCIE *(Sitting at the desk, her head in her hands)*

No one can accuse me of ruining him. I never asked him for anything.

JACQUES DURAND *(Whispering)*

Well, is he leaving you his little piece of property near Fécamp? . . . Because it seems, that's all he had left . . .

LUCIE *(Sadly)*

How should I know? That place is just a ruin, with an ordinary ocean view, and dark, cold rooms . . . Anyway, I am going to leave . . . *(She begins to cry again.)* Who could have told me that I would be leaving before the Grand Prix, and without poor Paul!

JACQUES DURAND

That's beyond our control! . . . *(Mechanically, he caresses her hair.)* Listen, my darling, you must compose yourself, be a lady. Doctor Godin is on his way, and perhaps the police . . . And then, their questions could upset you in the midst of your grief . . . Those kinds of people have no respect for great sadness . . . The hell of it is, they have to have the facts! Even if you were his widow . . . *(She makes a gesture of protest.)* No doubt, you are going to tell me that illicit love, just like the other kind, has its rights . . . *(Preoccupied)* Let's hope this madman made a proper will . . .

LUCIE *(Quickly)*

I'll find out right away. I can take care of myself, I've got a lawyer!

JACQUES DURAND

Ah! . . . *(A moment of silence. Frightened, they turn toward the corpse.)*

LUCIE

His mouth was so stiff! . . . Tomorrow morning, he will be really ugly, the poor man . . . He took poison, is that it?

JACQUES DURAND

Lucie, I assure you, it would be better for you to leave, before Godin gets here.

LUCIE *(With dignity)*

It's my duty. He believed that I loved him, I shall stay.

JACQUES DURAND

Have I offended you, my sweet? . . . Forgive me, I am not in my right mind, such a disaster . . . And the doctor is late . . . This silence around us . . . Come on, let's just talk, it will be

better . . . *(He goes near her.)* Lucie, will you allow me to be
your companion?

LUCIE *(Sitting up straight)*

Just like that, right away, before he is even buried? . . . Oh,
Monsieur Durand, you are completely wrong about me. We
could simply talk, I am a respectable girl.

JACQUES DURAND *(Quickly)*

Lucie, I meant nothing indecent. It is not a protector or a
guardian I am offering you: it's a friend . . . *(A pause)* And it is
Paul's friend, more than anyone else, who has the right to help
you through this ordeal . . . In any event, as I told you today, I
love you like my little sister . . . *(He hesitates.)* And if I held you
a little too close when I said this to you, here, in front of this
corpse *(He holds out his arms.)*, I offer you my apology.

LUCIE *(Taking his hand)*

You are so good . . . *(They both look at the corpse over their
shoulders.)* His eyes were so bright! . . .

JACQUES DURAND *(Making a face)*

Glassy, you mean . . .

LUCIE

This doctor will never come!

JACQUES DURAND *(Hurried)*

I'd like to go look for another one.

LUCIE *(Stands up and puts her arms around his neck.)*

And leave me alone, with this dead man? . . . Oh, Jacques,
Jacques! . . .

JACQUES DURAND *(Pressing her to him)*

Thank you. Now I know that you care for me. And if something could console me for the loss of a dear friend . . .

(They look at the corpse again.)

LUCIE

> We'll never laugh together again! . . . Dear Paul! He was really demented. There is no reason to lie about it anymore, it was almost ridiculous . . . He saw everything in black! . . . And the manias, the egotism . . .

JACQUES DURAND *(Quickly)*

> As for that, I agree. To go so far as killing himself without leaving me a word, me who loved him and felt sorry for him . . .

LUCIE

> It is true. He did forget you . . . But . . . *(She hesitates.)* he must have lent you money: he lent some to everyone, as a sort of a joke.

JACQUES DURAND *(Hesitating)*

> No . . . What he lent me before, I already paid back . . . *(There is noise behind the door.* LUCIE *jumps up in a panic. Jacques lets out a sigh, obviously relieved.)* It's the doctor.

*(*JEAN *enters, followed by* DOCTOR GODIN, *who puts his hat on the table then goes to the corpse.)*

Act Three, Scene Three

DOCTOR GODIN *(Removing his gloves)*

> He kept one cigar: the good one. We could not have predicted this contingency . . . In any case, I did not have the time to interrogate him . . . In sum, a very unpleasant affair . . . *(He notices Lucie and bows slightly.)* Madame . . . believe me, I understand your distress . . . I didn't see you at first . . . *(He lifts the cloth which covers the dead man's face.)* Poor boy, but what a malicious thing to do! . . . (LUCIE *leans her head on Jacques's shoulder, and* JACQUES *puts his arm around her waist.)* He is

still holding the end of his cigar between the index and the middle finger of his right hand . . . *(He examines the cigar and smells it.)* Of course! . . .

JEAN *(Pointing to Jacques and Lucie)*

Monsieur and Madame will be able to testify because they were the ones who found him dead . . . I thought he was sleeping . . . *(Sadly)* Oh, he was a strange master . . .

DOCTOR GODIN *(Examining the corpse)*

This man was built to live a hundred years, word of honor . . . They are obstinate, these neurotics . . . *(He stands up.)* Dartigny proceeded according to the following formula: my *nerium oleander* was inserted, with the help of a syringe, into the tip of the cigar . . . The alcohol evaporated, and the poison, well-spread in the tobacco leaves, retained all of its efficacy . . . The smoker's saliva dissolved it . . . *(Officiously)* A toxic dose is ten drops, twenty drops would be lethal . . . No screams, no pain, no vomiting, no great struggle . . . At first, a short period of excitation characterized by agitation, disquiet, constrictions of the thorax, anguish, then hallucinations of sight and hearing . . . Next the senses fail, the eyesight grows dim, the ears ring, the limbs weaken, the sick man collapses, several spasms occur, and a fainting fit ends the scene . . . A clean death. He chose a very distinguished mode of suicide . . . *(To Jacques Durand)* No family, eh?

JACQUES DURAND *(Respectful and a little stunned)*

An orphan, doctor. He didn't even have a distant cousin.

DOCTOR GODIN

That will simplify the situation . . . Then good causes and hospitals will inherit his estate? . . . Since you were intimate with him, you must know his intentions on this matter . . .

JACQUES DURAND

No, it is Mademoiselle.

(LUCIE *puts on her hat.*)

DOCTOR GODIN *(Bowing)*

Naturally.

LUCIE *(In a trembling voice)*

May I leave now?

JACQUES DURAND

You understand, doctor, she needs to pull herself together . . .
And I insist on going with her, because I am dying of hunger.
We will return after the usual preparations . . . *(Emphatically)*
Mademoiselle should not watch over this body. A justifiable
sense of decorum obliges her to leave . . . *(More loudly)* And I
agree.

DOCTOR GODIN *(Indifferent)*

A servant will suffice for the formalities. In any case . . . *(philosophically)* since there is no one else . . . *(He bows to Jacques and
Lucie, who go out rapidly.)*

Act Three, Scene Four

JEAN *(Very anxious)*

Does the doctor think that I will be interrogated?

DOCTOR GODIN *(Carefully placing the tip of the cigar in his brief-
case)*

I do not think so, my friend . . . *(After a moment's reflection)*
Now give me something to wash my hands.

(Curtain)

Appendix:
Rachilde's Plays

futurist Valentine de Saint-Point, April 1912; at Théâtre Michel
(La halte), 12 July 1912; at Notre Théâtre in Saint Petersburg,
July 1913, directed by Georges Pitoëff; and in other European
cities, according to one review.)

Volupté, Paris, Athénée-Comique, 4 May 1896

Le Panthère (prose poem), Paris, Théâtre Sarah Bernhardt, 25 February 1899

Le Meneur de Louves (lyric opera or ballet-pantomime, adapted or
co-authored by Pierre Hortala from the novel of the same title,
music by Jean Poueigh), Paris, offices of the *Mercure de France,*
7 January 1908. (Also in Paris, 11 March 1913; and at Maison
Gaveau, 21 April 1925, with the title *La Basilique aux
vainqueurs.*)

Le Char d'Apollon, Paris, Théâtre Antoine, 11 September 1913. (First
in a salon showing at the offices of the *Mercure de France,* 1913.)

La Poupée transparente, Paris, Renaissance (Art et Action), 9
December 1919. (First in a salon showing; also at the Théâtre
Albert I, 26 November 1920; and at the Athenée in Geneva,
June 1921.)

Le Rôdeur, Paris, Théâtre Fémina, 23 February 1928. (Also in Pittsburgh, 3 February 1994.)

Terreur (with G. Kamke), Paris, Grand Guignol, 30 September
1933

En deuil d'amour (with G. Kamke, adaptation of *Répulsion*), Paris,
Théâtre Potinière, 1 October 1933

La Tour d'amour (adaptation of novel, by Marcelle Maurette),
Paris, Grand Guignol, January 1935

Monsieur Vénus (adaptation of novel, by Pierre Spivikoff), Paris,
Théâtre des Mathurins, 10 February 1988

PUBLISHED

Un siècle après! (*L'Union Nontronnaise,* 21 November 1880;
reprinted Paris: Editions de Fourneau, 1985)

Scie (*Courrier de la Dordogne*, 10 March 1881; reprinted Paris: Editions de Fourneau, 1985)

Théâtre (Paris: Savine, 1891)

Le Démon de l'absurde (Paris: Mercure de France, 1894)

Contes et nouvelles suivis du théâtre (Paris: Mercure de France, 1900)

Le Char d'Apollon (*Comoedia*, 11 December 1913)

La Délivrance (*Mercure de France*, 1 July 1915)

La Poupée transparente (*Le Monde Nouveau*, 20 March 1919)

La Femme peinte (*Mercure de France*, 1 August 1921)

A l'auberge de l'aigle (*L'Age Nouveau*, 17 [July 1939]; reprinted Reims: A l'Ecart, 1977)

Rachilde: Opera teatrali (Mariangela Mazzocchi Doglio, *Miti e incanti nella Francia "Fin de siècle"* [Rome: Bulzoni, 1992])

UNPUBLISHED

Connais-tu l'amour? (with Alin Monjardin, 1899) (Bibliothèque de l'Arsenal)

Le Pape est disparu (n.d.) (Bibliothèque littéraire Jacques Doucet)

Les Fils d'Adam (n.d. [1894]) (Doucet)

Répulsion (n.d. [ca 1920]) (Doucet)

La Dernière aventure de tout-tuf-amon (n.d.) (Doucet)

Lui (n.d.) (Doucet)

L'Eclipse (with André David, 1924) (Doucet)

Library of Congress Cataloging-in-Publication Data

Rachilde, 1860–1953.

[Plays. English. Selections]

Madame La Mort and other plays / Rachilde ;
translated and edited by Kiki Gounaridou and
Frazer Lively ; introduction by Frazer Lively.

p.   cm. — (PAJ books)

ISBN 0-8018-5761-9 (hardcover : alk. paper). —
ISBN 0-8018-5762-7 (pbk. : alk. paper)

I. Gounaridou, Kiki. II. Lively, Frazer.
III. Title IV. Series.

PQ2643.A323A6   1998

842'.912—dc21   97-26493

                                        CIP